Lecture Notes of the Institute for Computer Sciences, Social Informatics and Telecommunications Engineering 494

The LNICST series publishes ICST's conferences, symposia and workshops.
LNICST reports state-of-the-art results in areas related to the scope of the Institute.
The type of material published includes

- Proceedings (published in time for the respective event)
- Other edited monographs (such as project reports or invited volumes)

LNICST topics span the following areas:

- General Computer Science
- E-Economy
- E-Medicine
- Knowledge Management
- Multimedia
- Operations, Management and Policy
- Social Informatics
- Systems

Carmela Comito · Domenico Talia

Editors

Pervasive Knowledge and Collective Intelligence on Web and Social Media

First EAI International Conference, PerSOM 2022
Messina, Italy, November 17–18, 2022
Proceedings

 Springer

Editors
Carmela Comito ⒾⒹ
ICAR-CNR
University of Calabria
Rende, Italy

Domenico Talia ⒾⒹ
University of Calabria
Rende, Italy

ISSN 1867-8211   ISSN 1867-822X (electronic)
Lecture Notes of the Institute for Computer Sciences, Social Informatics
and Telecommunications Engineering
ISBN 978-3-031-31468-1   ISBN 978-3-031-31469-8 (eBook)
https://doi.org/10.1007/978-3-031-31469-8

This Springer imprint is published by the registered company Springer Nature Switzerland AG
The registered company address is: Gewerbestrasse 11, 6330 Cham, Switzerland

Preface

We are delighted to introduce the proceedings of the first edition of the European Alliance for Innovation (EAI) International Conference on Pervasive Knowledge and Collective Intelligence on Web and Social Media - PerSoM 2022.

The conference was hosted during November 17–18, 2022 by the Institute for High Performance Computing and Networking of the Italian National Research Council (ICAR-CNR) and the DIMES department of the University of Calabria. The conference was held via online mode.

The Conference provided a setting for discussing recent developments, issues, challenges, opportunities and findings of research from different disciplines in the fields of Pervasive Computing, Web, and Social Media to promote ideas and practices about pervasive knowledge and collective intelligence in these fields. The conference targeted a wide variety of topics including new perspectives in social theories, complex networks, data science, knowledge management, web and social media.

The technical program of PerSoM 2022 consisted of 9 full papers from 35 submissions, each paper secured at least three double-blind reviews. The conference was organized in two sessions with oral presentation of the papers.

Coordination with the program chairs, Ester Zumpano and Paolo Trunfio, and with the Publicity chair Agostino Forestiero was essential for the success of the conference. We sincerely appreciate their constant support and guidance. It was also a great pleasure to work with such an excellent organizing committee team for their hard work in organizing and supporting the conference. In particular, the Technical Program Committee completed the peer-review process of technical papers and made a high-quality technical program. We are also grateful to the Conference Manager, Kristina Havlickova, for her support and to all the authors for contributing their research result to the conference.

We strongly believe that PerSoM 2022 provided a good forum for all researchers, developers and practitioners to discuss all science and technology aspects that are relevant to pervasive knowledge and collective intelligence on Web and Social Media. We also expect that future PerSoM conferences will be as successful and stimulating, as indicated by the contributions presented in this volume.

Carmela Comito
Domenico Talia

Organization

Steering Committee

Imrich Chlamtac	University of Trento, Italy
Carmela Comito	CNR-ICAR, Italy
Ester Zumpano	University of Calabria, Italy
Domenico Talia	University of Calabria, Italy

Organizing Committee

General Chair

Carmela Comito	CNR-ICAR, Italy

General Co-Chairs

Domenico Talia	University of Calabria, Italy
Shahab Shamshirband	National Yunlin University of Science and Technology, Taiwan

Technical Program Committee Chairs

Ester Zumpano	University of Calabria, Italy
Paolo Trunfio	University of Calabria, Italy
Andrea Calì	University of London, Birkbeck, UK
Huijan Wang	University of Technology, Delft, The Netherlands

Web Chairs

Luciano Caroprese	University of Calabria, Italy
David Manset	GNUBILA/MAAT, France

Publicity and Social Media Chairs

Annalisa Socievole	CNR-ICAR, Italy
Bruno Miguel Veloso	INESC TEC & University Portucalense & FEP University of Porto, Portugal

Sponsorship & Exhibits Chairs

Mauro Tropea	University of Calabria, Italy
Franco Cicirelli	CNR-ICAR, Italy

Publication Chair

Agostino Forestiero	CNR-ICAR, Italy

Local Chair

Eugenio Vocaturo	CNR-NANOTEC, Italy

Technical Program Committee

Technical Program Committee Chairs

Floriano De Rango	University of Calabria, Italy
Muhammad Imran	Qatar Computing Research Institute, Qatar
Mohamed Abd Elaziz	Zagazig University, Egypt

Technical Program Committee Members

Roberto Interdonato	University of Montpellier, France
Ali Mohammad Saghiri	Amirkabir University of Technology, Iran
Riccardo Pecori	University of Sannio, Italy
Ettore Ritacco	CNR-ICAR, Italy
David Manset	GNUBILA/MAAT, France
Laith Abualigah	Amman Arab University, Jordan
Kamran Gholizadeh HamlAbadi	University of Ottawa, Canada
Monireh Vahdati	University of Ottawa, Canada
Domenico Ursino	Università Politecnica delle Marche, Italy
Sanghoon Lee	Marshall University, USA

Elio Masciari	Università degli Studi di Napoli Federico II, Italy
Areeba Unair	Università degli Studi di Napoli Federico II, Italy
Geeta Rani	Manipal University Jaipur, India
Yazhou Zhang	Zhengzhou University of Light Industry, China
Francesco Cauteruccio	University of Calabria, Italy
Daniel Stamate	Goldsmith's University of London, UK
Bruno Miguel Veloso	INESC TEC & University Portucalense & FEP University of Porto, Portugal
Themis Palpanas	Data Intelligence Institute of Paris and University of Paris, France
Clara Pizzuti	CNR-ICAR, Italy
Sergio Flesca	University of Calabria, Italy
Rizos Sakellariou	University of Manchester, UK
Huijuan Wang	TU Delft, The Netherlands
Andrea Calì, Birkbeck	University of London, UK
Bruno Miguel Veloso	University of Porto, Portugal
Giancarlo Sperlì	Università degli Studi di Napoli Federico II, Italy
Silvia Chiusano	Politecnico di Torino, Italy
Genoveva Vargas Solar	LIG-LAFMIA, French Council of Scientific Research, France
Serena Pelosi	CNR-ICAR, Italy
Rosario Catelli	CNR-ICAR, Italy

Contents

Data Science

Assembling Fragments of Ancient Papyrus via Artificial Intelligence 3
  Eugenio Vocaturo and Ester Zumpano

Social Media Analysis and Mining

Misinformation and Disinformation on Social Media: An Updated Survey
of Challenges and Current Trends 17
  Fabrizio Lo Scudo

Topic Detection and Tracking in Social Media Platforms 41
  Riccardo Cantini and Fabrizio Marozzo

Fake News on Social Media: Current Research and Future Directions 57
  Luciano Caroprese, Carmela Comito, and Ester Zumpano

Incivility Balanced? Civil vs. Uncivil Speech in Online Political
Discussions as Dependent on Political Parallelism 65
  Daniil Volkovskii and Svetlana Bodrunova

Data and Network Security

Federated Learning for the Efficient Detection of Steganographic Threats
Hidden in Image Icons 83
  *Nunziato Cassavia, Luca Caviglione, Massimo Guarascio,
  Angelica Liguori, Giuseppe Surace, and Marco Zuppelli*

Machine Learning and Network Traffic to Distinguish Between Malware
and Benign Applications 96
  *Laith Abualigah, Sayel Abualigah, Mothanna Almahmoud,
  Agostino Forestiero, Gagan Sachdeva, and Essam S. Hanandeh*

Emerging Applications

A Comparative Study of the Coulomb's and Franklin's Laws Inspired
Algorithm (CFA) with Modern Evolutionary Algorithms for Numerical
Optimization   111
   Mojtaba Ghasemi, Mohsen Zare, Amir Zahedi, Rasul Hemmati,
   Laith Abualigah, and Agostino Forestiero

A Review of Space Exploration and Trajectory Optimization Techniques
for Autonomous Systems: Comprehensive Analysis and Future Directions   125
   Faiza Gul, Imran Mir, Uzma Gul, and Agostino Forestiero

Author Index   139

Data Science

Assembling Fragments of Ancient Papyrus via Artificial Intelligence

Eugenio Vocaturo[1,2]([✉]) [iD] and Ester Zumpano[1,2] [iD]

[1] DIMES, University of Calabria, Arcavacata, Italy
{e.vocaturo,e.zumpano}@dimes.unical.it
[2] CNR-Nanotec, Rende, CS, Italy

Abstract. The knowledge of humanity passes through the ancient texts whose acquisition, reconstruction and interpretation become tasks of fundamental importance. The simultaneous spread of equipment capable of exploiting new technologies for data acquisition together with the opportunities offered by Artificial Intelligence open new unimaginable horizons in different applications including the conservation of cultural heritage. In this work, we refer to the opportunity inherent the acquisition of texts from papyri via machine learning and deep learning applications. The theme of assembling fragments, will be investigated by referring to some recent interesting contributions of the scientific community.

Keywords: Artificial Intelligence · Ancient Papyrus Analysis · Assembling Fragment

1 Introduction

Archaeologists use ancient documents to investigate the organization of ancient human societies. In particular, the objective is to understand the customs, cultural, social and economic aspects of the daily life of the people who were alive at the time of the drafting of the documents. The discovery of manuscripts is always an extraordinary event that brings to light documents dating back many centuries ago. Manuscripts inevitably undergo a natural process of erosion aggravated by various other factors both related to the nature of the papyrus and the inks used and to atmospheric agents. Papyrus was one of the typical materials used since the dawn of time as a support for writing. Papyrus was a real revolution in ancient world science, and was produced using sophisticated techniques from the stems of the papyrus plant (Cyperus papyrus).

A unique type of paper is produced by extracting marrow threads from the stem and using them to create a specific pattern of warp and weft [36]. The ancient process of making this paper involved layering papyrus pith strips and gluing them together so that the strips in each layer are perpendicular to each other. The layers were then smoothed to achieve the desired surface finish and dried before being ready for writing [26]. The text was commonly written on

C. Comito and D. Talia (Eds.): PerSOM 2022, LNICST 494, pp. 3–13, 2023.
https://doi.org/10.1007/978-3-031-31469-8_1

the side of the papyrus with horizontal threads, named *Recto*, aligning with the thread lines, but in some cases, the back of the papyrus, named *Verso*, with vertical threads was also used for writing [6]. The production technique adopted involved local weaving patterns that characterized adjacent portions of the papyrus with a certain similarity [18] (Fig. 1).

Fig. 1. Structure of the Papyrus: horizontal threads (Recto) and vertical threads (Verso).

The way that papyri are made supports the idea that researchers who work with fragment alignment can rely on certain characteristics to match fragments. These researchers typically assume that fragments found in the same area will have similar visual features such as thread width, direction, spacing, and frequency. Analyzing the content of ancient papyri is challenging because it requires piecing together fragments of documents without knowing which fragments belong to the same document. This is similar to trying to complete a puzzle without knowing which pieces belong to which puzzle or if all the pieces are even present. With thousands of fragments from different documents, the task of reconstructing them can be time-consuming and labor-intensive. Recent opportunities offered by artificial intelligence allow the definition of support frameworks for the automatic reconstruction of ancient papyri (Fig. 2).

Fig. 2. Papyrus 27 of Ercolano.

Extreme challenges are faced in this domain, such as the management of the charred papyri of Herculaneum for which advanced approaches are being defined to simulate the virtual unrolling of papyri, which otherwise could not be treated. The bundles of papyrus rolls were scorched by the pyroclastic flows' tremendous heat during Vesuvius' eruption in 79 AD [1] (Fig. 3).

Fig. 3. Charred papyrus roll.

This intense overheating occurred in an extremely short period of time and in oxygen-poor environments, causing the rolls to carbonise into compact and extremely brittle blocks. Later they were covered and preserved by layers of extremely tenacious lava rock. Having to face these new challenges has prompted researchers to adopt new instruments for reading the papyri.

Terahertz time domain spectroscopic imaging (THz-TDSI) is an example of a non-destructive, non-ionizing measuring method that has lately been used to examine items from cultural heritage. In [25], the authors describe this method as well as the outcomes of non-contact measurements of papyrus texts, including pictures of concealed papyri. The historical binder, Arabic gum, and two typical pigments used to write ancient writings, carbon black and red ochre, were combined to create inks for current papyrus examples. The samples were scanned with a pulse with a spectral range between 0.1 and 1.5 THz in reflection at normal incidence. The depths of the layers are determined by the signals' temporal analysis, and the inks' frequency spectra are revealed by the signals' frequency spectra. In [5], the authors used an improved X-ray phase-contrast tomography non-destructive technology and a new set of numerical algorithms for "virtual - unrolling" to decipher several passages of text concealed inside carbonized Herculaneum papyri. In unopened scrolls, they were able to detect the greatest chunk of Greek text ever with previously unheard-of spatial resolution and contrast, all without causing any harm to these priceless ancient texts. The 'voice' of the Epicurean philosopher Philodemus is revived from Herculaneum papyri thanks to portions of the text that have been decrypted.

The paper is structured as follows: in Sect. 2 assembling fragments task will be recalled, referring to the related problems and to the first approaches with which the scientific community has begun to deal with the topic. In Sect. 3, we will refer to different machine learning and deep learning proposals, highlighting the strengths and weaknesses of the various proposals. The goal is to provide a meaningful overview for the reader who approaches to dealing with the issues of assembling fragments. Finally, in the last section we draw conclusions on the approaches and report specific open challenges to be faced.

2   Applications for Assembling Fragments

In this work, we refer to the opportunity inherent the acquisition of texts from papyri via artificial intellingence applications focusing to the particular issue of assembling fragments. The task of reconstructing a document by repositioning its fragments plays a key rule in archeology.

Given that two portions of various papyri might appear to be identical since they were written by the same person with the same ink and have a comparable level of wear, the challenges are especially pernicious. Because labeled data is uncommon, frequently uneven, unbalanced, and of irregular conservation statuses, it is difficult to automate using machine learning methods. However, the papyrology community has a real need for such software because manually reconstructing the papyri takes a lot of time and effort. Through artificial intelligence applications, the scientific community proposes solutions to overcome the manual coupling phases to assemble rolls as large and complete as possible.

In general, fragments of papyri that are discovered are often in poor condition due to degenerative processes such as erosion. Additionally, these fragments are typically very small and the writing on them is often scattered and fragmented: all these premises imply that pairing based on writing alone can easily fail: pairing based solely on geometric features, known as *pictorial approach*, is impractical.

The first works proposed by the scientific community, dating back to the 1960s,s, tried to use geometric features, such as shape, contours, curvature, of the fragments to be able to reconstruct the documents. The evolution of these approaches has resulted in proposals based on partial curve matching techniques that involve the use of only a small fraction of their boundaries [23]. However, the proposals based only on the exploitation of geometric features showed their limits when the documents to be recreated were large and the number of fragments to be recomposed is high.

A subsequent step for solving the puzzles dates back to the 90s, when greater importance was given [24] to the plot, scripts and drawings and also referring to the possibility of exploiting new metrics deriving from representation in different color spaces. In the study "Jigsaw puzzle solving using chromatic information" [17], the authors showed that incorporating color information can enhance the ability to solve puzzles by utilizing the color values of the boundary pixels and using them to match the boundary data of the image. The approach of exploiting the chromatic information of the points or of some sub-regions of the images in relation to those of the neighboring portions has given, among other things, important results in the analysis of images in the medical domain [19, 41, 42].

In recent years, drawing on the pool of opportunities of different machine learning and deep learning models, different solutions have been presented to combine archaeological fragments.

The authors of [38] provided a comprehensive approach for the color-based automatic reassembly of 2-D picture fragments. Four phases make up the proposed 2-D reassembly approach. Initially, approaches used in content-based image retrieval systems are used to identify picture fragments that are geographically nearby. The second procedure entails using a dynamic programming approach to locate the matching contour segments for each preserved pair of picture fragments. Finding the best transformation to align the appropriate border segments is the following step. The entire image is then pieced back together using its appropriately positioned components. The suggested approach was evaluated using digitally scanned photographs of ripped pieces of paper, and the results of the reassembly were quite good. Each step of the suggested technique might be improved by utilizing textual or semantic qualities in addition to color.

In [37], the authors describe a multipurpose method for figuring out the relationships between tiny pieces of ancient artifacts, such frescoes from the Bronze and Roman eras. The authors offer a collection of feature descriptors that are based not just on color and form but also on normal maps, in contrast to conventional 2D and 3D shape matching algorithms. These combine great data quality with discriminability and resistance against specific forms of degradation, and they are simple to gather. The new feature descriptors are easy to compute and match and vary from generic to domain-specific. The method was evaluated on three datasets of fresco pieces, illustrating how distinct trade-offs between efficiency and effectiveness result from multi-cue matching utilizing various subsets of features. The authors specifically show that 3D features are more discriminative than 2D or normal-based features, albeit at a greater computational cost, and that normal-based features are more effective than color-based features at equivalent computational complexity.

In [33],the authors use an unsupervised genetic algorithm to solve the search challenge by creating a collection of incomplete reconstructions that expands via recombination and selection over several generations. A new selection method that balances fitness and diversity in the population was developed for integrating incomplete reconstructions. This algorithm is resilient to noise and outliers. The suggested technique outperforms earlier automated systems in tests using a benchmark dataset by producing bigger and more precise global reconstructions. The weakness of this idea is that it lacks the strongest argument inherent in scarcity circumstances despite having dealt with nearly all enigmas.

The scarcity of samples and the complexity of the tasks to be tackled has so far constituted a great obstacle for effective proposals for correspondence of the papyrus. Some interesting proposals are based on the attempt to borrow image management techniques from other application contexts. In [30], Papy-S-Net is proposed for identify papyrus "spots" belonging to the same fragment. Through a Siamese neural network, which has two identical branches with shared weights during training and prediction, patches are coupled with intriguing outcomes (Fig. 4).

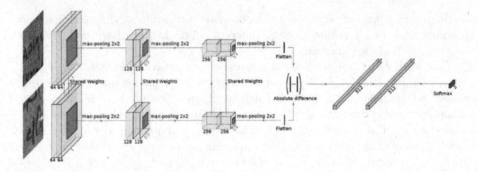

Fig. 4. The architecture of Papy-S-Net [30].

When input is given, each branch determines a functional vector. The input images are of size $128 \times 128 \times 3$, each pooling operation (red squares) divides the dimension of the images by 2, each convolution operation uses a kernel of size 3×3.

Everywhere in the method save the top layer-which utilizes Softmax for binary classification-relies on ReLU activation functions. The outputs from the two branches are merged by calculating the absolute value of the element-wise difference between each branch's flattened outputs. The weights of the two branches are shared. The Softmax two-layer fully-connected network is then given this vector: 500 papyrus pieces are used to train and evaluate the chosen network. The authors contrast Papy-S-findings Net's with a prior study by Koch et al. [22], which suggests a siamese network to correspond with written symbols. The extraction of patches from the papyrus pieces to form the ground truth was offered in order to train and validate the network. The suggested method was also tested in practice, with Papy-S-Net achieving 79% of accurate matches. This proposed approach is interesting even if the real challenge is the matching of fragments that exhibit a significant gaps between them. If on the one hand the outlines of the papyrus fragments are malformed, on the other hand their manufacturing technique allows to intercept pictorial information according to the pattern of the plots.

In [2], the authors presented an extremely intriguing solution: the algorithm is predicated on the idea that the thread patterns of papyrus have distinctive local characteristics, leading surrounding pieces to exhibit patterns resembling the threads' continuations. The suggested algorithm and system facilitate both the geometric alignment of the matched pairs of papyrus fragments against one another as well as the rapid and automatic categorization of the pairings. The concept is broken down into many phases and is based on machine learning and deep learning techniques. In order to discover thread continuation matches in the local edge regions (squares) between pairs of fragments, the challenge of matching fragments must first be broken down into smaller problems.

A convolutional neural network is used to solve this stage by ingesting raw pictures of the edge regions and providing local matching scores. By creating a complex voting system, the authors use these scores to draw conclusions regarding the matching of complete fragment pairings.

All of the information gathered from these processes is fed into a Random Forest classifier to create a higher order classifier that can determine whether a pair of fragments matches or not. The suggested technique was developed using a set of Dead Sea cave artifact fragments that were dated to the first century BCE. On a validation set with a similar origin, the algorithm displays great results (Fig. 5).

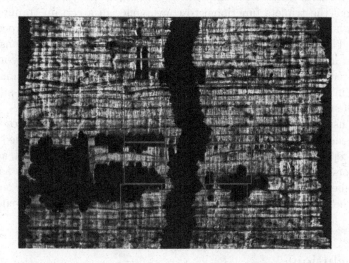

Fig. 5. Two adjacent artificially torn fragments with candidate squares for the matching phase [2]

The need to be able to dispose of discriminatory features with respect to the available data is pushing the community towards the adoption of deep learning models [27]. In general, also the number of classes in which the fragments will have to be classified is not known ex ante; therefore, the impossibility of using standard deep learning classification schemes suggested the adoption of deep metric learning (DML) methods.

In order to get a high score for two fragments from the same text and a low score for two fragments from separate documents, in [31] the authors employ a DML model. A comparable sample is considered to be near in terms of a metric geometric distance, such as the Euclidean distance, by the DML model, which learns the pertinent characteristics to be extracted and projects them into a latent space. As opposed to more "conventional" deep learning classification approaches, this method does not require knowledge of the number of classes in order to rebuild the document. The authors of this paper investigate how papyrologists can use Deep Convolutional Siamese-Networks to obtain useful matching suggestions on new data. They demonstrate that the from-scratch self-supervised approach is superior to using knowledge transfer from a large dataset, with the former attaining a top-1 accuracy score of 0.73 on an 800 fragment retrieval challenge.

In [20] the authors introduced a variant of Siamese networks known as Triplet Networks. This technique does away with similar and dissimilar pairings in favor of assigning the network a triplet made up of an Anchor sample, a positive sample, and a negative sample. In comparison to losses that take into account comparable and dissimilar samples individually, the optimization of a loss function based on the distance between Anchor/Positive and Anchor/Negative at each iteration enhances intra-class compactness and separability between classes [21]. By choosing the triplets functional to convergence in a certain training phase, the batch-hard and batch-all mining techniques enable learning process optimization. The availability of annotated data is not yet sufficient to ensure generalization in training deep learning models. This justifies why the community currently tends to adopt solutions that employ transfer learning or domain adaptation, as in [34,35], or that employ unsupervised learning [16], semi-supervised [32] or self-supervised [28,29].

When using self-supervised frameworks, trainable pretext activities are often initially generated from the raw unlabeled data. Models are compelled to learn practical representations related to the intended job by the pretext activities. The authors of [16], for instance, employ grouped SIFT descriptors as pretext activity labels to get the writer's name while retrieving information on papers. Instead, the authors of [29] train a model to reassemble mixed shredded text documents after producing disrupted documents.

3   Conclusion

Artificial intelligence applications are taking over in the cultural heritage community, resulting in the presentation of various proposals and sophisticated techniques for sensitive tasks such as those involving the activity of assembling fragments and more in general the recognition of historical documents [3,4,39]. We have examined some interesting proposals that adopt, from a methodological point of view, convolutional layer architectures capable of exploiting large amount of labeled data. Even the data sets that are gradually presented begin to be numerous and are made up of new types of documents from different areas of the world. The specificity of the contexts to be analyzed is stimulating the design of new architectures also using models initially proposed for other tasks in other fields. In general, deep learning-based methods show interesting performance.

The main challenge is the potential lack of diverse, reliable, and enough data needed to train deep learning models. Due to the unique characteristics of the documents, the analysis of historical documents is really an area of study that is defined by a relative lack or absence of good quality data.

The design of robust and scalable techniques for historical documents analysis seems to be the way that could give a breakthrough for artificial intelligence applications in this research area. It should not be underestimated that historical documents often also contain graphic information and numerical values.

The use of architectures developed in other research areas, such as the medical industry, where context-specific features [9] are exploited by machine learning algorithms [40,41], is a promising avenue that may be pursued. A significant barrier to the adoption of deep learning models is the requirement for vast amounts of training data, as well as the diminished explainability of the acquired findings and some level of skepticism among domain experts.

To this end a contribution in the direction of creating trusted and explainable AI and can be also provided by supporting machine learning framework with logic approaches [7,8,10] and adopting distributed techniques for data integration in cultural heritage domain [11–15].

In general, this is a typical criticality of deep learning models already encountered in other fields involving image analysis such as the medical one, where, for example, the results provided by frameworks based on deep learning models are viewed with great skepticism by specialists. Probably being able to identify a topic of interest could concentrate the community's efforts by pushing towards the creation of models that lend themselves to being generalized. T In general, the application of artificial intelligence models and techniques is destined to range even in contexts different from those of assembling fragments of ancient papyrus, thus giving new life to many research areas concerning the conservation of cultural heritage [3,4,39].

References

1. Iv. the herculaneum papyri. Bull. Inst. Class. Stud. **33**(S54), 36–45 (1986). https://doi.org/10.1111/j.2041-5370.1986.tb01374.x
2. Abitbol, R., Shimshoni, I., Ben-Dov, J.: Machine learning based assembly of fragments of ancient papyrus. J. Comput. Cult. Heritage (JOCCH) **14**(3), 1–21 (2021)
3. Berlino, A., Caroprese, L., La Marca, A., Vocaturo, E., Zumpano, E.: Augmented reality for the enhancement of archaeological heritage: a Calabrian experience. In: CEUR Workshop Proceedings, vol. 2320, pp. 86–94 (2019)
4. Berlino, A., Caroprese, L., Vocaturo, E., Zumpano, E.: A mobile application for the enhancement of POIs in Calabria. In: VIPERC@ IRCDL, pp. 13–25 (2020)
5. Bukreeva, I., et al.: Virtual unrolling and deciphering of Herculaneum papyri by x-ray phase-contrast tomography. Sci. Rep. **6**(1), 1–7 (2016)
6. Bülow-Jacobsen, A.: Writing materials in the ancient world (2011)
7. Calautti, M., Caroprese, L., Greco, S., Molinaro, C., Trubitsyna, I., Zumpano, E.: Existential active integrity constraints. Expert Syst. Appl. **168**, 114297 (2021). https://doi.org/10.1016/j.eswa.2020.114297
8. Caroprese, L., Trubitsyna, I., Truszczynski, M., Zumpano, E.: A measure of arbitrariness in abductive explanations. Theory Pract. Log. Program. **14**(4–5), 665–679 (2014). https://doi.org/10.1017/S1471068414000271
9. Caroprese, L., Vocaturo, E., Zumpano, E.: Features for melanoma lesions: extraction and classification. In: WI 2019, pp. 238–243. ACM (2019). https://doi.org/10.1145/3358695.3360898
10. Caroprese, L., Vocaturo, E., Zumpano, E.: Argumentation approaches for explanaible AI in medical informatics. Intell. Syst. Appl. **16**, 200109 (2022). https://doi.org/10.1016/j.iswa.2022.200109

11. Caroprese, L., Zumpano, E.: Aggregates and priorities in P2P data management systems. In: Desai, B.C., Cruz, I.F., Bernardino, J. (eds.) 15th International Database Engineering and Applications Symposium (IDEAS 2011), 21–27 September 2011, Lisbon, Portugal, pp. 1–7. ACM (2011). https://doi.org/10.1145/2076623.2076625
12. Caroprese, L., Zumpano, E.: Handling preferences in P2P systems. In: Lukasiewicz, T., Sali, A. (eds.) FoIKS 2012. LNCS, vol. 7153, pp. 91–106. Springer, Heidelberg (2012). https://doi.org/10.1007/978-3-642-28472-4_6
13. Caroprese, L., Zumpano, E.: Restoring consistency in P2P deductive databases. In: Hüllermeier, E., Link, S., Fober, T., Seeger, B. (eds.) SUM 2012. LNCS (LNAI), vol. 7520, pp. 168–179. Springer, Heidelberg (2012). https://doi.org/10.1007/978-3-642-33362-0_13
14. Caroprese, L., Zumpano, E.: A logic framework for P2P deductive databases. Theory Pract. Log. Program. **20**(1), 1–43 (2020). https://doi.org/10.1017/S1471068419000073
15. Caroprese, L., Zumpano, E.: Semantic data management in P2P systems driven by self-esteem. J. Log. Comput. **32**(5), 871–901 (2022). https://doi.org/10.1093/logcom/exac001
16. Christlein, V., Gropp, M., Fiel, S., Maier, A.: Unsupervised feature learning for writer identification and writer retrieval. In: 2017 14th IAPR International Conference on Document Analysis and Recognition (ICDAR), vol. 1, pp. 991–997. IEEE (2017)
17. Chung, M.G., Fleck, M.M., Forsyth, D.A.: Jigsaw puzzle solver using shape and color. In: ICSP 1998. 1998 Fourth International Conference on Signal Processing (Cat. No. 98TH8344), vol. 2, pp. 877–880. IEEE (1998)
18. Frösén, J.: Conservation of ancient papyrus materials (2011)
19. Fuduli, A., Veltri, P., Vocaturo, E., Zumpano, E.: Melanoma detection using color and texture features in computer vision systems. Adv. Sci. Technol. Eng. Syst. J. **4**(5), 16–22 (2019)
20. Hoffer, E., Ailon, N.: Deep metric learning using triplet network. In: Feragen, A., Pelillo, M., Loog, M. (eds.) SIMBAD 2015. LNCS, vol. 9370, pp. 84–92. Springer, Cham (2015). https://doi.org/10.1007/978-3-319-24261-3_7
21. Kaya, M., Bilge, H.Ş: Deep metric learning: a survey. Symmetry **11**(9), 1066 (2019)
22. Koch, G., Zemel, R., Salakhutdinov, R., et al.: Siamese neural networks for one-shot image recognition. In: ICML deep learning workshop, vol. 2, p. 0. Lille (2015)
23. Kong, W., Kimia, B.B.: On solving 2D and 3D puzzles using curve matching. In: Proceedings of the 2001 IEEE Computer Society Conference on Computer Vision and Pattern Recognition. CVPR 2001, vol. 2, pp. II-II. IEEE (2001)
24. Kosiba, D.A., Devaux, P.M., Balasubramanian, S., Gandhi, T.L., Kasturi, K.: An automatic jigsaw puzzle solver. In: Proceedings of 12th International conference on pattern recognition, vol. 1, pp. 616–618. IEEE (1994)
25. Labaune, J., Jackson, J., Duling, I., Menu, M., Mourou, G., et al.: Papyrus imaging with terahertz time domain spectroscopy. Appl. Phys. A **100**(3), 607–612 (2010)
26. Leach, B.: Papyrus manufacture. UCLA Encycl. Egyptology 1(1) (2009)
27. Lombardi, F., Marinai, S.: Deep learning for historical document analysis and recognition-a survey. J. Imaging **6**(10), 110 (2020)
28. Misra, I., Maaten, L.V.D.: Self-supervised learning of pretext-invariant representations. In: Proceedings of the IEEE/CVF Conference on Computer Vision and Pattern Recognition, pp. 6707–6717 (2020)
29. Paixão, T.M., et al.: Self-supervised deep reconstruction of mixed strip-shredded text documents. Pattern Recogn. **107**, 107535 (2020)

30. Pirrone, A., Aimar, M.B., Journet, N.: Papy-S-Net: a Siamese network to match papyrus fragments. In: Proceedings of the 5th International Workshop on Historical Document Imaging and Processing, pp. 78–83 (2019)
31. Pirrone, A., Beurton-Aimar, M., Journet, N.: Self-supervised deep metric learning for ancient papyrus fragments retrieval. Int. J. Doc. Anal. Recogn. (IJDAR) **24**(3), 219–234 (2021). https://doi.org/10.1007/s10032-021-00369-1
32. Romain, K., Abdel, B.: Semi-supervised learning through adversary networks for baseline detection. In: 2019 International Conference on Document Analysis and Recognition Workshops (ICDARW), vol. 5, pp. 128–133. IEEE (2019)
33. Sizikova, E., Funkhouser, T.: Wall painting reconstruction using a genetic algorithm. J. Comput. Cult. Heritage (JOCCH) **11**(1), 1–17 (2017)
34. Studer, L., et al.: A comprehensive study of ImageNet pre-training for historical document image analysis. In: 2019 International Conference on Document Analysis and Recognition (ICDAR), pp. 720–725. IEEE (2019)
35. Tang, Y., Peng, L., Xu, Q., Wang, Y., Furuhata, A.: CNN based transfer learning for historical Chinese character recognition. In: 2016 12th IAPR Workshop on Document Analysis Systems (DAS), pp. 25–29. IEEE (2016)
36. Thompson, E.M.: An Introduction to Greek and Latin Palaeography. Cambridge University Press, Cambridge (2013)
37. Toler-Franklin, C., Brown, B., Weyrich, T., Funkhouser, T., Rusinkiewicz, S.: Multi-feature matching of fresco fragments. ACM Trans. Graph. (TOG) **29**(6), 1–12 (2010)
38. Tsamoura, E., Pitas, I.: Automatic color based reassembly of fragmented images and paintings. IEEE Trans. Image Process. **19**(3), 680–690 (2009)
39. Vocaturo, E., Zumpano, E., Caroprese, L., Pagliuso, S.M., Lappano, D.: Educational games for cultural heritage. In: VIPERC@ IRCDL, pp. 95–106 (2019)
40. Vocaturo, E., Zumpano, E., Giallombardo, G., Miglionico, G.: DC-SMIL: a multiple instance learning solution via spherical separation for automated detection of displastyc nevi. In: IDEAS 2020, pp. 4:1–4:9. ACM (2020). https://doi.org/10.1145/3410566.3410611
41. Zumpano, E., Fuduli, A., Vocaturo, E., Avolio, M.: Viral pneumonia images classification by multiple instance learning: preliminary results. In: IDEAS 2021, pp. 292–296. ACM (2021)
42. Zumpano, E., et al.: Simpatico 3D mobile for diagnostic procedures. In: Proceedings of the 21st International Conference on Information Integration and Web-based Applications & Services, pp. 468–472 (2019)

Social Media Analysis and Mining

Misinformation and Disinformation on Social Media: An Updated Survey of Challenges and Current Trends

Fabrizio Lo Scudo$^{(\boxtimes)}$ [iD]

University of Calabria, Arcavacata, Italy
`fabrizio.loscudo@unical.it`

Abstract. Over the last decade, Social Media has been gradually shaping our world. From the Brexit to Ukraine war, passing through US election and COVID-19, there has been increasing attention on how social media affects our society. This attention has nowadays become an active research field in which researchers from different fields have proposed interdisciplinary solutions mainly aimed at fake news detection and prevention. Although this task is far to be solved.

Fake news detection is intrinsically hard since we have to cope with textual data; moreover the early detection requirement, to prevent wide diffusion, makes things even harder. If we now add a dynamic component to the problem definition we can easily understand why researchers have been keeping proposing new solutions to deal with new nuances of the problem. In this so fast-changing field, it is easy for newcomers to get lost. The scope of this work is not to provide a comprehensive review of the state-of-the-art approaches but instead a quick overview of the recent trends and how current technologies try to deal with the unresolved issues that characterize this task.

Keywords: Misinformation · Deep Learning · Social Media

1 Introduction

The advent of the Web2.0 [92] was introduced with a huge emphasis on collective culture and interoperability among end-users. The key change, compared to the previous generation, was the user-generated content which opened up endless opportunities for interacting and sharing information. But if this new feature has allowed the aggregation of people around common interests, facilitating the contamination of different cultures with healthy values and ethical principles, it also allows for the rapid dissemination of unsubstantiated rumors and incorrect interpretations which very often have often negatively impacted our society [37,91].

In general, the repercussions of bad information include opinion polarization, escalating fear and panic, weakening faith in scientific knowledge, historical negationism, or decreased access to health care. This was especially true during the

C. Comito and D. Talia (Eds.): PerSOM 2022, LNICST 494, pp. 17–40, 2023.
https://doi.org/10.1007/978-3-031-31469-8_2

COVID-19 pandemic since the fast spreading of misleading health information has increased vaccine hesitancy and delays in the provision of health care within population high-risk classes as shown in a recent WHO review [87]. The results of this work show the presence of much evidence that, during a crisis, the quality of the information tends to be low and that the development of adequate countermeasures, such as creating and promoting awareness campaigns, increase the amount of reliable content in mass media along with people's digital and health literacy, are needed. But since those policies require a huge amount of resources and time it is common practice to target the sources: the social media platforms.

Being social media platforms poorly regulated makes them nicely suitable for the task of spreading any kind of information. Of course not any kind of information is harmful to our society, and in this regard, it is useful to clarify the pieces of information we care about through the concept of *information disorder*. As described in [152], the notion of information disorder divides the alteration of information into three categories: mis-, dis-, and malinformation. With the term misinformation, we refer to false or inaccurate pieces of information, such as inaccurate dates, statistics, or translation errors whose degree of deliberately intended to deceive might be sometimes hard to assess. The same cannot be said for the idea of disinformation which is deliberately misleading or biased information, aimed to manipulate reality with narrative artifacts such as conspiracy theories, rumors, or simply propaganda. Finally, malinformation is explained as genuine (private) information about a person or corporate that is deliberately made public with the precise intent to cause harm: one famous example is the Russians hacked the Democrats' emails with the precise intent to unveil details to damage Clinton's reputation during her first presidential run.

This as many other definitions and classifications [54, 132] of the possible nature of or way to analyze the information present on social media, and more generally on the web, are useful in the matter of enhancing our understanding; but those concepts are hard to formalize in languages useful for the artificial intelligence as described in [80].

In the following sections we thus report useful insights in the process of formalizing the problem (Sect. 2), we highlight the challenges we have to deal with (Sect. 3), and list recent works that face these issues with deep learning techniques (Sect. 4). Finally, in Sect. 5 we try to describe what, from our point of view, are the most evident shortcomings and possible future research trends.

2   A Socio-technological Problem

Following [107, 108] the mis-/dis- information problem should be framed as a socio-technological one. This twofold view of the problem is something uncommon but it might be useful to design new operational features or indicators to be fed into algorithms.

In those works, authors propose a conceptual model, the disinformation and misinformation triangle, under which to capture key elements of harmful information and its spreading and propose interventions at a different level to detect and prevent that from happening. The model explains the spread of mis-/dis-information as the consequence of three causal factors which have to occur simultaneously to have a susceptible reader affected by harmful news which is propagating over social media. In this conceptual model, the factors of interest are the susceptible readers, the (un-)intentionally (false) information, and the medium by which the information reaches the readers.

Now, to prevent the diffusion and, as a consequence, the negative effect of the news on the readers, the authors propose three different kinds of interventions. The first concerns the automated identification of potentially harmful information which should support acts aimed to prevent its spreading. The second describes proactive educational campaigns to enhance a deeper critical judgment within the readers' minds. Third, a more structured legislative regulation of social media. But this last point should imply governments acts to push social media companies away from common marketing strategies [48] in favor of a more healthy society. Because of the complexity of discussing the acting at a legislative level, here we leave this aspect out in favor of a discussion about the first two components of the triangle: readers and information.

2.1 About Readers

In a recent work [74], authors try to highlight the importance of paying more attention to readers. The research questions posed in that study concern how the people, exposed to harmful information, would interpret it and which would be the right tools to intervene to prevent the negative effect. To answer those question authors extends a previous line of work on cognitive and ideologically motivated reasoning by introducing an aspect of information *familiarity*-vs-*novelty* to explain a major vulnerability when people are exposed to novel-vs-everyday news.

From a cognitive perspective, it seems that, in general, many individuals tend to rely on others' (possible famous ones') opinions to build their opinions[1] This form of *laziness* in the critical judgment process has been described in [94,95]. Those works suggest a certain inclination of such people towards believing fake news and such aspect is often exploited by mis-/dis- information makers to strengthen individuals' beliefs. In this regard, [31] highlights how people who experience a long exposition to fabricated information about a certain topic are more susceptible to strengthening their belief in that direction.

The ability to strengthen people's beliefs in a specific direction is the key to unlocking the real power behind mis-/dis- information. As it is shown in [60] stronger beliefs make easier the process of spreading the fake news, via *sharing* and *like*, as long as they match the beliefs. This in turn produces a process that amplifies the diffusion of the message allowing for a wider polarization [140]. At the basis of this phenomenon, there is the so-called *confirmation bias* [88], which is the condition in which people become more interested in the only news that is aligned with what they believe in. Overtime then people also become less

---

[1] Source: https://www.factcheck.org/2016/11/how-to-spot-fake-news/.

prone to challenge their beliefs with new information and only accept that that supports their views [82]. The analysis of this last point should however not be restricted to the mentioned conditions but should be also understood under the lens of ideologically motivated reasoning.

In [59] the author investigates the people's degree of acceptance of new information when they are exposed to a different political stimulus. In this study not only the acceptance but also the way, people process these new pieces of information is examined. The results show how ideological thinking lowered the people's acceptance level, restricting their interest to the only evidence that supports their own beliefs. Moreover, information processing in such contexts becomes lazier.

The discussion made so far might explain why certain people act irrationally while they are more inclined to misleading information. But it is worth noting that the majority of the cited works are based on exploratory studies due to the lack of theoretical guidance on this topic. Also, the described insights, being human-centered, do not find an easy spot within AI tools. For that reason, most of the research in the field only considers the information which is the topic of the next section.

2.2   About Information

In this section, we try to model the characteristics of mis-/dis-information that people may encounter online and how such a conceptual model can be used by AI systems. In this regard, we follow the conceptualization proposed in [80] which is used to facilitate the distinction among different types of information.

In [80] the authors use the term fake news as an umbrella term to start their analysis. This choice is motivated by the observation that over the years the term "fake news" has been used to refer to different types of content online regardless of whether it is intentional or not. This last distinction is important since the concept of fake news is very often tied to the idea of deceitful intent [5]. An example of that might be the results in [14] which show as reliable news outlets such as The New York Times, The Washington Post, and Associated Press were involved in disseminating false information. The authors of [80] thus propose a taxonomy of online content designed to identify signature features of fabricated news. With this taxonomy, they try to cover the nuances behind the definition of misinformation and also to extend its coverage to contents that are not intended for informational purposes, such as satirical expressions, commentary, or citizen journalism. The taxonomy is made of eight categories for the domain of fake news: real news, false news, polarized content, satire, misreporting, commentary, persuasive information, and citizen journalism. Each of these categories is characterized by unique features describing linguistic properties, sources, intentions, structural components, and network characteristics. Among these categories, we here focus on the difference between real and fake news and refer the readers to [80] for further details.

In general, recognizing fake news is a difficult task since it requires a consistent mental effort from readers who should use common-sense and background knowledge to assess the veracity [66]. However, although false news tries to imitate real information in its form, they often lack the news media's editorial style and references of reliable sources. So we could be tempt to use topic-specific characteristics, impartiality, and objectivity as indicators to understand the message's nature. For example, objectivity could be verified with tools for fact-checking and quote verification, described later, whereas impartiality might be verified by an analysis of sources and attributions [123]. Stylistic indicators, instead, are subtler to define since they are made by particular lexical and syntactical structures [7]. The real news should be written with a peculiar journalistic style [33] and moreover, it should lack any storytelling characteristics [123].

For example, the typical false news headlines have to catch the readers' attention straightforwardly and in a specific way, thus they are very often characterized by complete claims which makes them longer than real news ones [50]. This kind of engagement is similar to the technique called *click-bait* in which the user is tempted to follow/click on the link associated with the headline to read more about a specific event. Of course, the primary goal of this technique is not to spread misinformation but to advertise revenues. However news of that kind has also shown a low level of veracity [126].

Other than the mentioned features also moral-emotional words can be a suitable indicator since their presence could indicate low content veracity. As shown in [20] messages with moral-emotional language spread much faster.

Finally, besides the employed features one last distinction could be made on the amount of text considered in the analysis. The analysis with the least amount of information, that is claim-level methods [23,47,96], through medium size or article-level methods [51,98], to large amount of text that characterizes source-level methods [53,130].

The focus of the above-mentioned studies, regardless of the amount of the used information, is to build automated tools aimed to detect fake. We will discuss the fact-checking problem in the next section and later what are recent works on this topic.

3   Challenges

3.1   Fact-Checking

Without taking into account emotional and ideological aspects, we can say that assessing whether the news is true is a cognitively laborious process. In this process an individual, before accepting new evidence as facts, try to verify its reliability, truthfulness, and independence [17]. This becomes even more complicated in a highly dynamic environment in which new information is produced at an unprecedented rate under the need of engaging always larger audiences [77]. This has led to the launch of numerous fact-checking organizations, such as FactCheck[2], PolitiFact[3] and NewsGuard[4] and many others.

---

[2] https://www.factcheck.org/.

[3] https://www.politifact.com/.

[4] https://www.newsguardtech.com/.

The majority of these examples are based on laborious manual fact-checking which consist of a series of procedure, for example, identifying the claim, gathering evidence, check source credibility, which represents the cognitive effort required by the reader to assess the truthfulness of the news. However, manual validation only covers a small portion of the daily-produced new information. For this reason automatic fact-checking has been attracting attention in the context of computational journalism before [32,38] and within artificial intelligence community later [45,165]. In the AI field, especially, thanks to the advent of deep learning techniques the research on automated fact-checking has made important progress [40,158]. New insights in the fields of natural language processing (NLP) and information retrieval (IR) have allowed us to process large-scale textual information with increasing accuracy to assess the truthfulness of a claim. For example, in [141] authors design a pipeline to identify claims (to be checked), find appropriate evidence, and produce judgments. From there many datasets, systems, and simpler models for fact-checking were presented RumourEval [27], CLEF CheckThat [13], and ClaimBuster [47]. Those approaches share common components to verify web documents such as document retrieval, claim spotters, and claim validity checker. Other systems, such as FEVER2 [138] and SCIVER [145], are only designed to tackle claim validation under the assumption that claims are provided and worthy to be checked.

In general, once it is provided new information, automated fact-checking can be thought of as a four stages process, or sub-tasks:

1. **Claim detection and matching**: typically identified as the first step, this sub-task aims to identify claims that require verification [46] which is similar to the practices of journalistic fact-checking [18]. It also involves questions related to assessing the check-worthy of a claim [86] and how this worthiness varies over time [12]. Recently, [61] propose a model called Claim/not Claim, built on top of InferSent embeddings [24], with which pose attention to the question of whether or not a claim can be verifiable with the readily available evidence. Correlated with the claim detection there is the claim matching problem which is often framed as a ranking task and involves the retrieval of already checked facts w.r.t. the similarity with the fact to check [119] from some sort of database [93].

2. **Evidence retrieval**: its scope is to find sources supporting or refuting the claim. First attempts to solve the fact-checking task were based only on claims and pattern-recognition approaches without taking in account external knowledge [103,143,149]. Without supporting evidence, such attempts struggled to evaluate well-presented misinformation [116]. Nowadays, if we consider the quality of automatic text-generation tools, it is very difficult to distinguish between real news and fake news by only focusing on the style [157]. On the other side, the choice made by those works were dictated by the fundamental issue which is that not always possible to get access to trustful information. The methods, that try to include external knowledge sources, very often to assess the veracity of a claim postulate the access to trusted sources, such as encyclopedias, other media, or external knowledge bases [11,122,131,135].

This assumption were needed since, in general, assessing the trustfulness of a source and later verify a claim is a demanding task [68].

3. **Claim verification**: in this step based on the retrieved/available evidences researchers formulate the task as a classification problem. The outputs for this classification task ranges from a simple binary classification [84,96] to multi-class classification in which labels represent degrees of truthfulness [3,11,120]. By taking in account the well-known limitations, the multi-class setting is in general to prefer since the challenges of supporting strong position are very often hard to handle.

4. **Justification production**: this task concerns the production of human-interpretable explanations, or at least a set of evidence, supporting the classification decision. As discussed in [139] it is important, from a journalistic point of view, to convince readers of what the claim is saying. In the simplest case, we can start by presenting the evidence returned by a retrieval system. For example, in [70] authors build a justification employing an attention signal to highlight the salient parts of the retrieved information. However, more recent works have focused on the generation of textual justifications, as documented in [62], in which the system produces a summary as a proxy to explain its decision process [9]. However, although the created summary provides useful insights about how the model works, it misses to clarify the exact inference procedure; a possible solution to this issue might be relying on symbolic systems in which the justification is automatically produced as a result of the logical-inference process [1,34].

The description made so far allows us only to introduce a few concepts along with interesting works in the field. The methods present in the literature are much more and several works try to provide an exhaustive overview of the subject, such as [85,133], while [126,165] have more focus on social media.

3.2 Degrees of Truthfulness, Falsehood, and Subjectivity

Even with enough amount of information it could be not so easy to assess the truthfulness or the falsehood of a claim. In general, stories may be technically accurate but still misleading. In [8], for example, authors build a system for detecting cherry-picking to measure the amount of support a story has since it is not so rare to present well-chosen evidence to support misleading news. Since not all its information might be equally trustworthy, it is better to avoid considering a claim as a whole. Works that divide the veracity check among different sources [155] and that assess the agreement among those [161] are less prone to misclassify a claim although they still require improvements. Furthermore, new methods should however face a challenging problem which is subjective in the judgment process.

The degree of truthfulness or falsehood eventually has to do with a subjective interpretation of the reality. This interpretation is conditioned by the audience's social/cultural and religious system and education background. This last point allows us to introduce the next challenge which discusses the complexity of the annotation process while creating coherent datasets.

3.3   Datasets Building

State-of-the-art systems for the claim-related task and misinformation detection
heavily rely on training large language models. Those models, although pre-
trained on large-scale textual corpora, still require large and high-quality labeled
datasets to be fine-tuned to the fake news task. Despite the recent research
efforts, the available datasets are often synthetic, highly imbalanced in favor of
fake news samples, and biased. For example, using crowd-sourcing based techniques datasets, as discussed for the more general task of reading comprehension
in [49,153], easily conduct to biased models as documented for the related task
of natural language inference NLI[5] in [43,76].

In the context of fact-checking, [117] highlighted the effect of claim-
representative keywords on the predictions of models trained upon the dataset
FEVER [136]. Adversarial training was proposed in the context of the FEVER
2 shared task [138] as an attempt to solve this issue. Other solutions to mitigate
biases are based on making models less susceptible to catastrophic forgetting
[73,134]. Finally, authors in [114] try to make models more sensitive to subtle
differences in supporting evidence by building better contrastive samples.

The imbalance of datasets is another major source of issues since models
trained on such datasets with a high chance tend to overfit. For example, [154]
tries to alleviate this issue with a resampling procedure that involve only the
samples of the minority class.

In the following of this section, we try to report a non-exhaustive list of the
most commonly used datasets in the field of misinformation and disinformation.
However, since each dataset has unique features and differences in the annotation
process synthesizing all the datasets' nuances in a few lines would be misleading.
We prefer to report the summary in the form of a simple table and provide the
reference to the original paper to further details.

Claim-Related Dataset. For the claim-oriented datasets, we split the summary into two tables. In Table 1 on the top, we report datasets that were built
to predict check-worthy claims in which the typical input is social media post
with textual content. While in Table 1 on the bottom the datasets for claim
validation.

Multimodal Dataset. In Table 2 we report a short list of most of the existing
multi-modal datasets. Those datasets have recently become quite popular since
the evolution of social media platforms which enhanced their text-based forums
with multi-modal environments. This happened since visual modalities such as
images and videos are more favorable and attractive to the users. As consequence
misinformation producers have heavily relied on contextual correlations between
modalities such as text and image. In Table 2, WS_O_TRN_TP stands for the
ensemble of content providers: Wall Street, Onion, TheRealNews, and ThePoke.

---

[5] NLI is the task of determining whether a text h, the hypothesis, can (logically) be
inferred from a given text p, called premise [19].

Table 1. In the top table, we report the claim detection datasets, where we split the datasets into two categories: Worthy Assessment and Checkable. Below is the table of claim validation datasets which are expressed in terms of factual verification.

Dataset for Worthy Assessment	Input Size	Num. Classes	Sources
CredBank [79]	1k	5	Twitter
Weibo [72]	5k	2	Twitter/Weibo
Suspicious [144]	131k	2/5	Twitter
CheckThat20-T1 [13]	8k	Ranking	Twitter
CheckThat21-T1A [86]	17k	2	Twitter
Debate [46]	1k	3	Transcript
ClaimRank [36]	5k	Ranking	Transcript
Dataset for Checkable	Input Size	Num. Classes	Sources
CitationReason [105]	4k	13	Wikipedia
PolitiTV [61]	6k	7	Transcript
SemEval19-TA[78]	2k	3	Forum

Dataset for Factual Verification	Input Size	Evidence	Num. Classes	Source
StatsProperties [142]	7k	KG[a]	Numeric	Internet
CreditAssess [97]	5k	Text	2	Fact Check/Wiki
PunditFact [104]	4k	-	2/6	Fact Check
Liar [150]	12k	Meta	6	Fact Check
Liar-Plus [4]	12k	Text/Meta	6	Fact Check
FEVER [136]	185k	Text	3	Wiki
NELA [52]	136k	-	2	News
BuzzfeedNews [99]	1k	Meta	4	Facebook
BuzzFace [111]	2k	Meta	4	Facebook
FakeNewsNet [125]	23,196	Meta	2	Fact Check
Snopes [44]	6k	Text	3	Fact Check
MultiFC [10]	36k	Text/Meta	2-27	Fact Check
Climate-FEVER [28]	1k	Text	4	Climate
SciFact [146]	1k	Text	3	Science
PUBHEALTH [62]	11k	Text	4	Fact Check
COVID-Fact [109]	4k	Text	2	Forum
TabFact [22]	92k	Table	2	Wiki
InfoTabs [42]	23k	Table	3	Wiki
HOVER [56]	26k	Text	2	Wiki
WikiFactCheck [112]	124k	Text	2	Wiki
FakeCovid [120]	5k	-	2	Fact Check
X-Fact [41]	31k	Text	7	Fact Check
AnswerFact [160]	60k	Text	5	Amazon
VitaminC [115]	488k	Text	3 Classes	Wiki
Sem-Tab-Fact [148]	5k	Table	3	Wiki
FEVEROUS [6]	87k	Text/Table	3	Wiki

[a] Stands for Knowledge Graph

Table 2. In this table we report the fake news datasets characterized by multi-modal input.

Dataset for Factual Verification	Input Size	Num. Classes	Modalities	Source
image-verification-corpus [16]	17k	2	image,text	Twitter
Fakeddit [83]	1M	2,3,6	image,text	Reddit
NewsBag [57]	215k	2	image, text	WS_O_TRN_TP
NewsBag++ [57]	589k	2	image,text	WS_O_TRN_TP
MM-COVID [69]	11,173	2	image,text,social context	Twitter
ReCOVery [164]	2,029	2	text,image	Twitter
CoAID [25]	5,216	2	image,text	Twitter
MMCoVaR [21]	2k articles+24k tweets	2	image,text,social context	Twitter
N24News [151]	60k	24	image,text	New York Times
MuMiN [90]	10k	3	image,text	Twitter

Although over recent years there has been an increasing interest in such kinds of multi-modal datasets there are still data-related challenges. The first, and perhaps most important, is the lack of comprehensive datasets since many datasets are small in size and often imbalanced in favor of fake examples. Other current flaws are the mono-lingual nature of most of them and the limited heterogeneity of their content (w.r.t. images and text of the articles). This last point becomes more apparent when we consider that many datasets are built to only cover a specific event, such as COVID-19 or elections. In this regard, only the recent Mumin Dataset [90] tries to address some of the issues just mentioned.

The Large-Scale Multilingual Multi-modal Fact-Checked Misinformation Social Network Dataset (MuMin) is quite large since it comprises 26 thousand Twitter threads (roughly 20M tweets). These threads have been aligned to 13 thousand fact-checked claims which, besides the labels, provide further information about the context than that contained in the tweets. Finally, the authors have chosen a conservative approach for the annotation strategy: if the claim is *mostly true* then it is labeled as factual, whereas when it is *half true* or *half false* it is labeled as misinformation. In this way, they collapse the claims' multi-class labeling into a binary choice under the assumption that the presence of a significant part of false information within a claim should expose the readers to misleading content.

4   Current Research Trends

Recent trends in the field of misinformation and disinformation detection largely rely on deep learning techniques. The common strategies can be divided into two major categories. The first is to use a pipeline whose components could be pre-trained large models or not. The pipeline's components are usually trained independently and evaluate each input separately. The second option is a joint distribution-based approach in which the output distribution is a function of multiple components. In the following, we discuss some solutions for the claim-related task and the misinformation detection with multi-modal inputs.

4.1   Claim-Related Tasks Solutions

Claim detection is an essential part of automated fact-checking systems as all other components need to rely on the output of this stage. Its goal is to select claims that need to be checked later in the pipeline. The task of claim detection, like many other tasks, has however the intrinsic issue related to the volume of data produced on a daily base. In this scenario, researchers have been trying not to use external evidence and frame the problem as a classification task.A binary decision is made on whether each input sentence constitutes a claim or not. Typically, a set of sentences is given as input.

The early systems were characterized by hand-crafted platform-dependent features such as Reddit karma and up-votes [2] or Twitter metadata [29]. Others approach relied on linguistic features or entities recognized in the text [167], and syntactic ones [163]. More recently, deep learning-based methods have taken hand-crafted features over. Recurrent and Graph neural networks have over time proved their value in this context. Especially the possibility of introducing user's activity context information [166] has allowed them to build more accurate models [39]. Graph Neural Networks has also provided a solid framework to model propagation behavior of (potentially harmful) claims [81,156].

Collecting evidence supporting or undermining a claim is a task that was typically carried out using consolidated indexing technologies, such as Lucene[6], and entity linking based on some knowledge bases [121]. For example in [137] authors use a pipeline, made of an evidence retrieval module and a verification module, in which a combination of TF-IDF for document retrieval and string matching using named entities and capitalized expressions was used. Advance in the field of embedding representations for textual input has later opened up the possibility of employing vectors as the element on which to compute similarity [58] and indexing [67]. Also, better methods for text generation have allowed to [30]'s authors to use an approach based on question-generated answering to provide information, in the form of natural language briefs about the claim before performing the check. In [65] authors propose to use language models as fact-checkers, but later works have shown as this approach might be prone to propagate the biases of the language models into the new task [64].

Something missing in all the above-mentioned methods it the lack of reasoning over multiple pieces of evidence. Of course, introducing a reasoning component into a differentiable system is not an easy task. The first attempt, for example, was based on the simple concatenation of different piece of evidence [71,89]. But more recent ones try to aggregate information from different evidence in a more elaborated way. [113] uses a joint reranking-and-verification model to fuses evidence documents, [162] uses semantic role labeling and graph structure to re-define the relative distances of words that, along with graph convolutional network and graph attention network, propagate and aggregate information from neighboring nodes on the graph.

Approaches for justification production could be based on attention to highlighting the span within the evidence [70,124]. However, later works [55,100,118]

---

[6] https://lucene.apache.org/.

have shown as removing high-score tokens may sometimes leave unaltered the final justification while low-score ones could heavily affect the results. In the opposite direction the research in [1, 34] rely on logical languages to provide more robust methods. Those methods are essentially rule-based approaches with the constraint of representation power of the formalism. They employ a triplet-based format for the knowledge to guarantee scalability but, at the same time, limit the kind of information that can be stored in the knowledge base. Finally, following a recent trend, authors in [62] use a generative method, based on an abstractive approach, to provide a textual justification. However, as shown in [75], there is a chance that such an approach could generate misleading explanations due to hallucination phenomena.

4.2 Multi-Modal Misinformation Detection

Combinations of features e.g., text and image have been recently used to enhance the performance of misinformation detection systems. Different fusion mechanisms can be implemented, but most of them can be classified into early and late fusion. In early fusion, all the different kinds of features are fed into one model in their original form. The result will be later passed to the classifier as shown in [35]. Later fusion, on the other hand, performs the fusion on the extracted features provided by different components. Often features, such as text, images, and social networks are concatenated into a single vector that feeds the classifier [102, 106, 127]. However, it seems that simple concatenation is not very effective to build meaningful representations. In the attempt to generate better representation attention mechanism was used.

Different variants of attention have been proposed. For example, the Hierarchical Multi-modal Contextual Attention Networks [101] uses a hierarchical structural bias for the attention modules to extract more meaningful information. [110] propose a shared cross attention transformer encoder which, thanks to the shared layers, tries to learn correlations among modalities. Another cross-modal attention Residual system is presented in [128] aims to selectively extract the relevant information for a target modality from other modalities while preserving its distinctive features. Other examples of attention mechanism for misinformation detection are [63, 70, 147]. Besides the attention mechanism, the other most common types of neural architecture used for fake news detection are Graph Neural Networks (GNNs).

GNNs have gained huge success in recent years. [129] introduces a temporal propagation-based fake news detection framework in which structure, content semantics, and temporal information are used to recognize temporal evolution patterns of real-world news. By incorporating information from the medical knowledge graph DETERRENT [26] uses a GNN and an attention mechanism to build knowledge-guided article embeddings which are used for misinformation detection. Finally, [159] builds a deep diffusive network model to learn the representations of news articles, creators, and subjects simultaneously. These representations should incorporate the network structure information thanks to the connections among news articles, creators, and news subjects.

The last work we discuss is [15], which uses a continual learning approach for engagement prediction of a user in spreading misinformation. The authors propose an ego-graphs replay strategy in continual learning which is a different perspective compared to the work mentioned before. Ego-graphs are simple graphs composed of a single central node (an user) and its neighbors. Based on this kind of representation and using graph neural networks authors can predict whether users will engage in misinformation and conspiracy theories spreading. Also, the catastrophic forgetting issue related to the dynamic nature of online social networks is addressed with a continual learning approach.

5   Conclusion

In this study, we tried to give an updated not-exhaustive review of the state of the mis- and disinformation research field. We framed the problem as a socio-technological one and provided references to important works in the fields of psychology, journalism, and cognitive science. We paid particular attention to these aspects because any proposed solutions should take into account the way we, as humans, process information and how that information can be affected by deceptive intentions of other individuals.

We strongly believe that future high-quality datasets will continue to help progress the field if they succeed to have less biased content. This can be achieved with a multi-disciplinary approach and, of course, with some technological assistance. AI tools from natural language processing (NLP) and machine learning (ML) are advancing very quickly and can help, but the adoption of any tool should be carefully evaluated. Also corporate, such as Twitter, Facebook, YouTube, and Instagram, plays a critical role in this context since they are very often the medium through which potentially-dangerous information is spread. More regulated principles should guide those platforms.

The last point, which opens up a different discussion, regards how the challenges of this automation process concerning governance, accountability, and censorship would eventually impact our right to free speech.

References

1. Ahmadi, N., Lee, J., Papotti, P., Saeed, M.: Explainable fact checking with probabilistic answer set programming. arXiv preprint arXiv:1906.09198 (2019)
2. Aker, A., Derczynski, L., Bontcheva, K.: Simple open stance classification for rumour analysis. arXiv preprint arXiv:1708.05286 (2017)
3. Alhindi, T., Petridis, S., Muresan, S.: Where is your evidence: improving fact-checking by justification modeling. In: Proceedings of the first workshop on fact extraction and verification (FEVER), pp. 85–90 (2018)
4. Alhindi, T., Petridis, S., Muresan, S.: Where is your evidence: improving fact-checking by justification modeling. In: Proceedings of the First Workshop on Fact Extraction and VERification (FEVER), pp. 85–90. Association for Computational Linguistics, Brussels, Belgium (2018). https://doi.org/10.18653/v1/W18-5513, https://www.aclweb.org/anthology/W18-5513

5. Allcott, H., Gentzkow, M.: Social media and fake news in the 2016 election. J. Econ. Perspect. **31**(2), 211–36 (2017)
6. Aly, R., et al.: FEVEROUS: fact extraction and verification over unstructured and structured information. In: 35th Conference on Neural Information Processing Systems (NeurIPS 2021) Track on Datasets and Benchmarks (2021)
7. Argamon-Engelson, S., Koppel, M., Avneri, G.: Style-based text categorization: what newspaper am i reading. In: Proceedings of the AAAI Workshop on Text Categorization, pp. 1–4 (1998)
8. Asudeh, A., Jagadish, H.V., Wu, Y., Yu, C.: On detecting cherry-picked trend-lines. Proc. VLDB Endow. **13**(6), 939–952 (2020)
9. Atanasova, P., Simonsen, J.G., Lioma, C., Augenstein, I.: Generating fact checking explanations. arXiv preprint arXiv:2004.05773 (2020)
10. Augenstein, I., et al.: MultiFC: a real-world multi-domain dataset for evidence-based fact checking of claims. In: Proceedings of the 2019 Conference on Empirical Methods in Natural Language Processing and the 9th International Joint Conference on Natural Language Processing (EMNLP-IJCNLP), pp. 4685–4697. Association for Computational Linguistics, Hong Kong, China (2019). https://doi.org/10.18653/v1/D19-1475, https://www.aclweb.org/anthology/D19-1475
11. Augenstein, I., et al.: MultiFC: a real-world multi-domain dataset for evidence-based fact checking of claims. arXiv preprint arXiv:1909.03242 (2019)
12. Barnoy, A., Reich, Z.: The when, why, how and so-what of verifications. Journal. Stud. **20**(16), 2312–2330 (2019)
13. Barrón-Cedeño, A., et al.: Overview of CheckThat! 2020: automatic identification and verification of claims in social media. In: Arampatzis, A., et al. (eds.) CLEF 2020. LNCS, vol. 12260, pp. 215–236. Springer, Cham (2020). https://doi.org/10.1007/978-3-030-58219-7_17
14. Benkler, Y., Faris, R., Roberts, H.: Network Propaganda: Manipulation, Disinformation, and Radicalization in American Politics. Oxford University Press, Oxford (2018)
15. Bo, H., McConville, R., Hong, J., Liu, W.: Ego-graph replay based continual learning for misinformation engagement prediction. arXiv preprint arXiv:2207.12105 (2022)
16. Boididou, C., Papadopoulos, S., Zampoglou, M., Apostolidis, L., Papadopoulou, O., Kompatsiaris, Y.: Detection and visualization of misleading content on twitter. Int. J. Multimed. Inf. Retr. **7**(1), 71–86 (2018)
17. Borden, S.L., Tew, C.: The role of journalist and the performance of journalism: ethical lessons from "fake" news (seriously). J. Mass Media Ethics **22**(4), 300–314 (2007)
18. Borel, B.: The Chicago Guide to Fact-Checking. University of Chicago Press, Chicago (2016)
19. Bowman, S.R., Angeli, G., Potts, C., Manning, C.D.: A large annotated corpus for learning natural language inference. arXiv preprint arXiv:1508.05326 (2015)
20. Brady, W.J., Wills, J.A., Jost, J.T., Tucker, J.A., Van Bavel, J.J.: Emotion shapes the diffusion of moralized content in social networks. Proc. Natl. Acad. Sci. **114**(28), 7313–7318 (2017)
21. Chen, M., Chu, X., Subbalakshmi, K.: MMCoVaR: multimodal COVID-19 vaccine focused data repository for fake news detection and a baseline architecture for classification. In: Proceedings of the 2021 IEEE/ACM International Conference on Advances in Social Networks Analysis and Mining, pp. 31–38 (2021)

22. Chen, W., et al.: TabFact: a large-scale dataset for table-based fact verification. In: 8th International Conference on Learning Representations, ICLR 2020. Addis Ababa, Ethiopia (2020). https://openreview.net/forum?id=rkeJRhNYDH

23. Ciampaglia, G.L., Shiralkar, P., Rocha, L.M., Bollen, J., Menczer, F., Flammini, A.: Computational fact checking from knowledge networks. PLoS ONE **10**(6), e0128193 (2015)

24. Conneau, A., Kiela, D., Schwenk, H., Barrault, L., Bordes, A.: Supervised learning of universal sentence representations from natural language inference data. arXiv preprint arXiv:1705.02364 (2017)

25. Cui, L., Lee, D.: CoAID: COVID-19 healthcare misinformation dataset. arXiv preprint arXiv:2006.00885 (2020)

26. Cui, L., Seo, H., Tabar, M., Ma, F., Wang, S., Lee, D.: DETERRENT: knowledge guided graph attention network for detecting healthcare misinformation. In: Proceedings of the 26th ACM SIGKDD International Conference on Knowledge Discovery & Data Mining, pp. 492–502 (2020)

27. Derczynski, L., et al.: SemEVAL-2017 task 8: RumourEVAL: determining rumour veracity and support for rumours. arXiv preprint arXiv:1704.05972 (2017)

28. Diggelmann, T., Boyd-Graber, J.L., Bulian, J., Ciaramita, M., Leippold, M.: CLIMATE-FEVER: a dataset for verification of real-world climate claims. CoRR **abs/2012.00614** (2020). https://arxiv.org/abs/2012.00614

29. Enayet, O., El-Beltagy, S.R.: NileTMRG at SemEVAL-2017 task 8: determining rumour and veracity support for rumours on Twitter. In: Proceedings of the 11th International Workshop on Semantic Evaluation (SemEval-2017), pp. 470–474 (2017)

30. Fan, A., et al.: Generating fact checking briefs. arXiv preprint arXiv:2011.05448 (2020)

31. Fazio, L.: Pausing to consider why a headline is true or false can help reduce the sharing of false news. Harvard Kennedy School Misinformation Review 1(2) (2020)

32. Flew, T., Spurgeon, C., Daniel, A., Swift, A.: The promise of computational journalism. Journal. Pract. **6**(2), 157–171 (2012)

33. Frank, R.: Caveat lector: fake news as folklore. J. Am. Folk. **128**(509), 315–332 (2015)

34. Gad-Elrab, M.H., Stepanova, D., Urbani, J., Weikum, G.: ExFaKT: a framework for explaining facts over knowledge graphs and text. In: Proceedings of the Twelfth ACM International Conference on Web Search and Data Mining, pp. 87–95 (2019)

35. Gallo, I., Ria, G., Landro, N., La Grassa, R.: Image and text fusion for UPMC food-101 using BERT and CNNs. In: 2020 35th International Conference on Image and Vision Computing New Zealand (IVCNZ), pp. 1–6. IEEE (2020)

36. Gencheva, P., Nakov, P., Màrquez, L., Barrón-Cedeño, A., Koychev, I.: A context-aware approach for detecting worth-checking claims in political debates. In: 2017 Proceedings of the International Conference Recent Advances in Natural Language Processing, RANLP, pp. 267–276 (2017)

37. George, J.F., Gupta, M., Giordano, G., Mills, A.M., Tennant, V.M., Lewis, C.C.: The effects of communication media and culture on deception detection accuracy. MIS Q. **42**(2), 551–575 (2018)

38. Graves, D.: Understanding the promise and limits of automated fact-checking (2018)

39. Guo, H., Cao, J., Zhang, Y., Guo, J., Li, J.: Rumor detection with hierarchical social attention network. In: Proceedings of the 27th ACM International Conference on Information and Knowledge Management, pp. 943–951 (2018)
40. Guo, Z., Schlichtkrull, M., Vlachos, A.: A survey on automated fact-checking. Trans. Assoc. Comput. Linguist. **10**, 178–206 (2022)
41. Gupta, A., Srikumar, V.: X-fact: A new benchmark dataset for multilingual fact checking. In: Proceedings of the 59th Annual Meeting of the Association for Computational Linguistics and the 11th International Joint Conference on Natural Language Processing (Volume 2: Short Papers), pp. 675–682 (2021)
42. Gupta, V., Mehta, M., Nokhiz, P., Srikumar, V.: INFOTABS: inference on tables as semi-structured data. In: Proceedings of the 58th Annual Meeting of the Association for Computational Linguistics, pp. 2309–2324. Association for Computational Linguistics (2020). https://doi.org/10.18653/v1/2020.acl-main.210, https://www.aclweb.org/anthology/2020.acl-main.210
43. Gururangan, S., Swayamdipta, S., Levy, O., Schwartz, R., Bowman, S.R., Smith, N.A.: Annotation artifacts in natural language inference data. arXiv preprint arXiv:1803.02324 (2018)
44. Hanselowski, A., Stab, C., Schulz, C., Li, Z., Gurevych, I.: A richly annotated corpus for different tasks in automated fact-checking. In: Proceedings of the 23rd Conference on Computational Natural Language Learning (CoNLL), pp. 493–503. Association for Computational Linguistics, Hong Kong, China (2019). https://doi.org/10.18653/v1/K19-1046, https://www.aclweb.org/anthology/K19-1046
45. Hassan, N., et al.: The quest to automate fact-checking. In: Proceedings of the 2015 Computation+ Journalism Symposium (2015)
46. Hassan, N., Li, C., Tremayne, M.: Detecting check-worthy factual claims in presidential debates. In: Proceedings of the 24th ACM International on Conference on Information and Knowledge Management, pp. 1835–1838 (2015)
47. Hassan, N., et al.: ClaimBuster: the first-ever end-to-end fact-checking system. Proc. VLDB Endow. **10**(12), 1945–1948 (2017)
48. He, S., Hollenbeck, B., Proserpio, D.: The market for fake reviews. Mark. Sci. **41**, 896–921 (2022)
49. Hermann, K.M., et al.: Teaching machines to read and comprehend. In: Advances in Neural Information Processing Systems, vol. 28 (2015)
50. Horne, B.D., Adali, S., Sikdar, S.: Identifying the social signals that drive online discussions: a case study of reddit communities. In: 2017 26th International Conference on Computer Communication and Networks (ICCCN), pp. 1–9. IEEE (2017)
51. Horne, B.D., Dron, W., Khedr, S., Adali, S.: Assessing the news landscape: a multi-module toolkit for evaluating the credibility of news. In: 2018 Companion Proceedings of the The Web Conference, pp. 235–238 (2018)
52. Horne, B.D., Khedr, S., Adali, S.: Sampling the news producers: a large news and feature data set for the study of the complex media landscape. In: Proceedings of the Twelfth International Conference on Web and Social Media, ICWSM 2018, Stanford, California, USA, 25-28 June 2018, pp. 518–527. AAAI Press (2018). https://aaai.org/ocs/index.php/ICWSM/ICWSM18/paper/view/17796
53. Horne, B.D., Nevo, D., O'Donovan, J., Cho, J.H., Adalı, S.: Rating reliability and bias in news articles: does AI assistance help everyone?. In: Proceedings of the International AAAI Conference on Web and Social Media, vol. 13, pp. 247–256 (2019)
54. Jack, C.: Lexicon of lies: terms for problematic information. Data Soc. **3**(22), 1094–1096 (2017)

55. Jain, S., Wallace, B.C.: Attention is not explanation. arXiv preprint arXiv:1902.10186 (2019)
56. Jiang, Y., Bordia, S., Zhong, Z., Dognin, C., Singh, M., Bansal, M.: HoVer: a dataset for many-hop fact extraction and claim verification. In: Findings of the Association for Computational Linguistics: EMNLP 2020, pp. 3441–3460. Association for Computational Linguistics (2020). https://doi.org/10.18653/v1/2020.findings-emnlp.309, https://www.aclweb.org/anthology/2020.findings-emnlp.309
57. Jindal, S., Sood, R., Singh, R., Vatsa, M., Chakraborty, T.: NewsBag: a multimodal benchmark dataset for fake news detection. In: CEUR Workshop Proceedings, vol. 2560, pp. 138–145 (2020)
58. Johnson, J., Douze, M., Jégou, H.: Billion-scale similarity search with GPUs. IEEE Trans. Big Data 7(3), 535–547 (2019)
59. Kahan, D.M.: Ideology, motivated reasoning, and cognitive reflection: an experimental study. Judgm. Decis. Mak. 8, 407–24 (2012)
60. Kim, J., Tabibian, B., Oh, A., Schölkopf, B., Gomez-Rodriguez, M.: Leveraging the crowd to detect and reduce the spread of fake news and misinformation. In: Proceedings of the Eleventh ACM International Conference on Web Search and Data Mining, pp. 324–332 (2018)
61. Konstantinovskiy, L., Price, O., Babakar, M., Zubiaga, A.: Toward automated factchecking: developing an annotation schema and benchmark for consistent automated claim detection. Digit. threats: Res. Pract. 2(2), 1–16 (2021)
62. Kotonya, N., Toni, F.: Explainable automated fact-checking: a survey. arXiv preprint arXiv:2011.03870 (2020)
63. Kumari, R., Ekbal, A.: AMFB: attention based multimodal factorized bilinear pooling for multimodal fake news detection. Expert Syst. Appl. 184, 115412 (2021)
64. Lee, N., Bang, Y., Madotto, A., Khabsa, M., Fung, P.: Towards few-shot fact-checking via perplexity. arXiv preprint arXiv:2103.09535 (2021)
65. Lee, N., Li, B.Z., Wang, S., Yih, W.t., Ma, H., Khabsa, M.: Language models as fact checkers? arXiv preprint arXiv:2006.04102 (2020)
66. Lewandowsky, S., Ecker, U.K., Cook, J.: Beyond misinformation: understanding and coping with the "post-truth" era. J. Appl. Res. Mem. Cogn. 6(4), 353–369 (2017)
67. Lewis, P., et al.: Retrieval-augmented generation for knowledge-intensive NLP tasks. In: Advanced in Neural Information Processing System, vol. 33, pp. 9459–9474 (2020)
68. Li, Y., et al.: A survey on truth discovery. ACM SIGKDD Explor. Newsl. 17(2), 1–16 (2016)
69. Li, Y., Jiang, B., Shu, K., Liu, H.: MM-COVID: a multilingual and multimodal data repository for combating COVID-19 disinformation. arXiv preprint arXiv:2011.04088 (2020)
70. Lu, Y.J., Li, C.T.: GCAN: graph-aware co-attention networks for explainable fake news detection on social media. arXiv preprint arXiv:2004.11648 (2020)
71. Luken, J., Jiang, N., de Marneffe, M.C.: QED: a fact verification system for the fever shared task. In: Proceedings of the First Workshop on Fact Extraction and VERification (FEVER), pp. 156–160 (2018)
72. Ma, J., et al.: Detecting rumors from microblogs with recurrent neural networks. In: Kambhampati, S. (ed.) Proceedings of the Twenty-Fifth International Joint Conference on Artificial Intelligence, IJCAI 2016, New York, NY, USA, 9–15 July 2016, pp. 3818–3824. IJCAI/AAAI Press (2016). http://www.ijcai.org/Abstract/16/537

73. Mahabadi, R.K., Belinkov, Y., Henderson, J.: End-to-end bias mitigation by modelling biases in corpora. arXiv preprint arXiv:1909.06321 (2019)

74. Manikonda, L., Nevo, D., Horne, B.D., Arrington, C., Adali, S.: The reasoning behind fake news assessments: a linguistic analysis. AIS Trans. Human-Comput. Interact. **14**(2), 230–253 (2022)

75. Maynez, J., Narayan, S., Bohnet, B., McDonald, R.: On faithfulness and factuality in abstractive summarization. In: Proceedings of the 58th Annual Meeting of the Association for Computational Linguistics, pp. 1906–1919. Association for Computational Linguistics (2020). https://doi.org/10.18653/v1/2020.acl-main.173, https://aclanthology.org/2020.acl-main.173

76. McCoy, R.T., Pavlick, E., Linzen, T.: Right for the wrong reasons: diagnosing syntactic heuristics in natural language inference. arXiv preprint arXiv:1902.01007 (2019)

77. Mihailidis, P., Viotty, S.: Spreadable spectacle in digital culture: civic expression, fake news, and the role of media literacies in "post-fact" society. Am. Behav. Sci. **61**(4), 441–454 (2017)

78. Mihaylova, T., Karadzhov, G., Atanasova, P., Baly, R., Mohtarami, M., Nakov, P.: SemEval-2019 task 8: Fact checking in community question answering forums. In: Proceedings of the 13th International Workshop on Semantic Evaluation, pp. 860–869. Association for Computational Linguistics, Minneapolis, Minnesota, USA (2019). https://doi.org/10.18653/v1/S19-2149, https://www.aclweb.org/anthology/S19-2149

79. Mitra, T., Gilbert, E.: CREDBANK: A large-scale social media corpus with associated credibility annotations. In: Cha, M., Mascolo, C., Sandvig, C. (eds.) Proceedings of the Ninth International Conference on Web and Social Media, ICWSM 2015, University of Oxford, Oxford, UK, 26–29 May 2015, pp. 258–267. AAAI Press (2015). http://www.aaai.org/ocs/index.php/ICWSM/ICWSM15/paper/view/10582

80. Molina, M.D., Sundar, S.S., Le, T., Lee, D.: "fake news" is not simply false information: a concept explication and taxonomy of online content. Am. Behav. Sci. **65**(2), 180–212 (2021)

81. Monti, F., Frasca, F., Eynard, D., Mannion, D., Bronstein, M.M.: Fake news detection on social media using geometric deep learning. arXiv preprint arXiv:1902.06673 (2019)

82. Moravec, P., Minas, R., Dennis, A.R.: Fake news on social media: people believe what they want to believe when it makes no sense at all. Kelley School of Business research paper (18–87) (2018)

83. Nakamura, K., Levy, S., Wang, W.Y.: r/Fakeddit: a new multimodal benchmark dataset for fine-grained fake news detection. arXiv preprint arXiv:1911.03854 (2019)

84. Nakashole, N., Mitchell, T.: Language-aware truth assessment of fact candidates. In: Proceedings of the 52nd Annual Meeting of the Association for Computational Linguistics (Volume 1: Long Papers), pp. 1009–1019 (2014)

85. Nakov, P., et al.: Automated fact-checking for assisting human fact-checkers. arXiv preprint arXiv:2103.07769 (2021)

86. Nakov, P., et al.: The CLEF-2021 CheckThat! lab on detecting check-worthy claims, previously fact-checked claims, and fake news. In: Hiemstra, D., Moens, M.-F., Mothe, J., Perego, R., Potthast, M., Sebastiani, F. (eds.) ECIR 2021. LNCS, vol. 12657, pp. 639–649. Springer, Cham (2021). https://doi.org/10.1007/978-3-030-72240-1_75

87. Borges do Nascimento, I.J., et al.: Infodemics and health misinformation: a systematic review of reviews. Bull. World Health Org. **100**(9), 544–561 (2022)
88. Nickerson, R.S.: Confirmation bias: a ubiquitous phenomenon in many guises. Rev. Gen. Psychol. **2**(2), 175–220 (1998)
89. Nie, Y., Chen, H., Bansal, M.: Combining fact extraction and verification with neural semantic matching networks. In: Proceedings of the AAAI Conference on Artificial Intelligence, vol. 33, pp. 6859–6866 (2019)
90. Nielsen, D.S., McConville, R.: MuMiN: a large-scale multilingual multimodal fact-checked misinformation social network dataset. In: Proceedings of the 45th International ACM SIGIR Conference on Research and Development in Information Retrieval, pp. 3141–3153 (2022)
91. Olan, F., Jayawickrama, U., Arakpogun, E.O., Suklan, J., Liu, S.: Fake news on social media: the impact on society. Inf. Syst. Front., 1–16 (2022). https://doi.org/10.1007/s10796-022-10242-z
92. O'reilly, T.: What is Web 2.0. "O'Reilly Media Inc", Sebastopol (2009)
93. Passaro, L.C., Bondielli, A., Lenci, A., Marcelloni, F.: UNIPI-NLE at CheckThat! 2020: approaching fact checking from a sentence similarity perspective through the lens of transformers. In: CLEF (Working Notes) (2020)
94. Pennycook, G., Rand, D.G.: Lazy, not biased: Susceptibility to partisan fake news is better explained by lack of reasoning than by motivated reasoning. Cognition **188**(-), 39–50 (2019)
95. Pennycook, G., Rand, D.G.: The psychology of fake news. Trends Cogn. Sci. **25**(5), 388–402 (2021)
96. Popat, K., Mukherjee, S., Strötgen, J., Weikum, G.: Credibility assessment of textual claims on the web. In: Proceedings of the 25th ACM International on Conference on Information and Knowledge Management, pp. 2173–2178 (2016)
97. Popat, K., Mukherjee, S., Strötgen, J., Weikum, G.: Credibility assessment of textual claims on the web. In: Mukhopadhyay, S., et al. (eds.) Proceedings of the 25th ACM International Conference on Information and Knowledge Management, CIKM 2016, Indianapolis, IN, USA, 24–28 Oct 2016, pp. 2173–2178. ACM (2016). https://doi.org/10.1145/2983323.2983661
98. Potthast, M., Kiesel, J., Reinartz, K., Bevendorff, J., Stein, B.: A stylometric inquiry into hyperpartisan and fake news. arXiv preprint arXiv:1702.05638 (2017)
99. Potthast, M., Kiesel, J., Reinartz, K., Bevendorff, J., Stein, B.: A stylometric inquiry into hyperpartisan and fake news. In: Proceedings of the 56th Annual Meeting of the Association for Computational Linguistics (Volume 1: Long Papers), pp. 231–240. Association for Computational Linguistics, Melbourne, Australia (2018). https://doi.org/10.18653/v1/P18-1022, https://www.aclweb.org/anthology/P18-1022
100. Pruthi, D., Gupta, M., Dhingra, B., Neubig, G., Lipton, Z.C.: Learning to deceive with attention-based explanations. In: Proceedings of the 58th Annual Meeting of the Association for Computational Linguistics, pp. 4782–4793 (2020)
101. Qian, S., Wang, J., Hu, J., Fang, Q., Xu, C.: Hierarchical multi-modal contextual attention network for fake news detection. In: Proceedings of the 44th International ACM SIGIR Conference on Research and Development in Information Retrieval, pp. 153–162 (2021)
102. Raj, C., Meel, P.: ARCNN framework for multimodal infodemic detection. Neural Netw. **146**, 36–68 (2022)
103. Rashkin, H., Choi, E., Jang, J.Y., Volkova, S., Choi, Y.: Truth of varying shades: analyzing language in fake news and political fact-checking. In: Proceedings of

the 2017 Conference on Empirical Methods in Natural Language Processing, pp. 2931–2937 (2017)

104. Rashkin, H., Choi, E., Jang, J.Y., Volkova, S., Choi, Y.: Truth of varying shades: analyzing language in fake news and political fact-checking. In: Proceedings of the 2017 Conference on Empirical Methods in Natural Language Processing, pp. 2931–2937. Association for Computational Linguistics, Copenhagen, Denmark (2017). https://doi.org/10.18653/v1/D17-1317, https://www.aclweb.org/anthology/D17-1317

105. Redi, M., Fetahu, B., Morgan, J.T., Taraborelli, D.: Citation needed: a taxonomy and algorithmic assessment of Wikipedia's verifiability. In: Liu, L., et al. (eds.) The World Wide Web Conference, WWW 2019, San Francisco, CA, USA, 13–17 May 2019, pp. 1567–1578. ACM (2019). https://doi.org/10.1145/3308558.3313618

106. Rezayi, S., Soleymani, S., Arabnia, H.R., Li, S.: Socially aware multimodal deep neural networks for fake news classification. In: 2021 IEEE 4th International Conference on Multimedia Information Processing and Retrieval (MIPR), pp. 253–259. IEEE (2021)

107. Rubin, V.L.: Disinformation and misinformation triangle: a conceptual model for "fake news" epidemic, causal factors and interventions. J. Documentation **75**, 1013–1034 (2019)

108. Rubin, V.L.: Misinformation and Disinformation: Detecting Fakes with the Eye and AI. Springer Nature, Berlin (2022)

109. Saakyan, A., Chakrabarty, T., Muresan, S.: COVID-Fact: Fact extraction and verification of real-world claims on COVID-19 pandemic. In: Zong, C., Xia, F., Li, W., Navigli, R. (eds.) Proceedings of the 59th Annual Meeting of the Association for Computational Linguistics and the 11th International Joint Conference on Natural Language Processing, ACL/IJCNLP 2021, (Volume 1: Long Papers), Virtual Event, 1–6 Aug 2021, pp. 2116–2129. Association for Computational Linguistics (2021). https://doi.org/10.18653/v1/2021.acl-long.165, https://doi.org/10.18653/v1/2021.acl-long.165

110. Sachan, T., Pinnaparaju, N., Gupta, M., Varma, V.: SCATE: shared cross attention transformer encoders for multimodal fake news detection. In: Proceedings of the 2021 IEEE/ACM International Conference on Advances in Social Networks Analysis and Mining, pp. 399–406 (2021)

111. Santia, G.C., Williams, J.R.: BuzzFace: a news veracity dataset with Facebook user commentary and egos. In: Proceedings of the Twelfth International Conference on Web and Social Media, ICWSM 2018, Stanford, California, USA, 25–28 June 2018, pp. 531–540. AAAI Press (2018). https://aaai.org/ocs/index.php/ICWSM/ICWSM18/paper/view/17825

112. Sathe, A., Ather, S., Le, T.M., Perry, N., Park, J.: Automated fact-checking of claims from wikipedia. In: Calzolari, N., et al. (eds.) Proceedings of The 12th Language Resources and Evaluation Conference, LREC 2020, Marseille, France, 11–16 May 2020, pp. 6874–6882. European Language Resources Association (2020). https://aclanthology.org/2020.lrec-1.849/

113. Schlichtkrull, M., Karpukhin, V., Oğuz, B., Lewis, M., Yih, W.t., Riedel, S.: Joint verification and reranking for open fact checking over tables. arXiv preprint arXiv:2012.15115 (2020)

114. Schuster, T., Fisch, A., Barzilay, R.: Get your vitamin C! robust fact verification with contrastive evidence. arXiv preprint arXiv:2103.08541 (2021)

115. Schuster, T., Fisch, A., Barzilay, R.: Get your Vitamin C! robust fact verification with contrastive evidence. In: Proceedings of the 2021 Conference of the North

American Chapter of the Association for Computational Linguistics: Human Language Technologies, pp. 624–643. Association for Computational Linguistics (2021). https://www.aclweb.org/anthology/2021.naacl-main.52

116. Schuster, T., Schuster, R., Shah, D.J., Barzilay, R.: The limitations of stylometry for detecting machine-generated fake news. Comput. Linguist. **46**(2), 499–510 (2020)

117. Schuster, T., Shah, D.J., Yeo, Y.J.S., Filizzola, D., Santus, E., Barzilay, R.: Towards debiasing fact verification models. arXiv preprint arXiv:1908.05267 (2019)

118. Serrano, S., Smith, N.A.: Is attention interpretable? In: Proceedings of the 57th Annual Meeting of the Association for Computational Linguistics, pp. 2931–2951 (2019)

119. Shaar, S., Martino, G.D.S., Babulkov, N., Nakov, P.: That is a known lie: detecting previously fact-checked claims. arXiv preprint arXiv:2005.06058 (2020)

120. Shahi, G.K., Nandini, D.: FakeCovid–a multilingual cross-domain fact check news dataset for COVID-19 (2020)

121. Shen, W., Wang, J., Han, J.: Entity linking with a knowledge base: issues, techniques, and solutions. IEEE Trans. Knowl. Data Eng. **27**(2), 443–460 (2014)

122. Shi, B., Weninger, T.: Discriminative predicate path mining for fact checking in knowledge graphs. Knowl.-Based Syst. **104**, 123–133 (2016)

123. Shoemaker, P.J.: News values: reciprocal effects on journalists and journalism. Int. Encycl. Media Effects, 1–9 (2017)

124. Shu, K., Cui, L., Wang, S., Lee, D., Liu, H.: Defend: explainable fake news detection. In: Proceedings of the 25th ACM SIGKDD International Conference on Knowledge Discovery & Data Mining, pp. 395–405 (2019)

125. Shu, K., Mahudeswaran, D., Wang, S., Lee, D., Liu, H.: FakeNewsNet: a data repository with news content, social context, and spatiotemporal information for studying fake news on social media. Big Data **8**(3), 171–188 (2020). https://doi. org/10.1089/big.2020.0062

126. Shu, K., Sliva, A., Wang, S., Tang, J., Liu, H.: Fake news detection on social media: a data mining perspective. ACM SIGKDD Explor. Newsl. **19**(1), 22–36 (2017)

127. Singhal, S., Shah, R.R., Chakraborty, T., Kumaraguru, P., Satoh, S.: SpotFake: a multi-modal framework for fake news detection. In: 2019 IEEE Fifth International Conference on Multimedia Big Data (BigMM), pp. 39–47. IEEE (2019)

128. Song, C., Ning, N., Zhang, Y., Wu, B.: A multimodal fake news detection model based on crossmodal attention residual and multichannel convolutional neural networks. Inf. Process. Manage. **58**(1), 102437 (2021)

129. Song, C., Shu, K., Wu, B.: Temporally evolving graph neural network for fake news detection. Inf. Process. Manage. **58**(6), 102712 (2021)

130. Starbird, K., Arif, A., Wilson, T., Van Koevering, K., Yefimova, K., Scarnecchia, D.: Ecosystem or echo-system? Exploring content sharing across alternative media domains. In: Proceedings of the International AAAI Conference on Web and Social Media, vol. 12 (2018)

131. Syed, Z.H., Röder, M., Ngomo, A.-C.N.: Unsupervised discovery of corroborative paths for fact validation. In: Ghidini, C., et al. (eds.) ISWC 2019. LNCS, vol. 11778, pp. 630–646. Springer, Cham (2019). https://doi.org/10.1007/978-3-030-30793-6_36

132. Tandoc Jr., E.C., Lim, Z.W., Ling, R.: Defining "fake news" a typology of scholarly definitions. Digit. Journal. **6**(2), 137–153 (2018)

133. Thorne, J., Vlachos, A.: Automated fact checking: task formulations, methods and future directions. arXiv preprint arXiv:1806.07687 (2018)

134. Thorne, J., Vlachos, A.: Elastic weight consolidation for better bias inoculation. arXiv preprint arXiv:2004.14366 (2020)

135. Thorne, J., Vlachos, A., Christodoulopoulos, C., Mittal, A.: Fever: a large-scale dataset for fact extraction and verification. arXiv preprint arXiv:1803.05355 (2018)

136. Thorne, J., Vlachos, A., Christodoulopoulos, C., Mittal, A.: FEVER: a large-scale dataset for fact extraction and verification. In: Proceedings of the 2018 Conference of the North American Chapter of the Association for Computational Linguistics: Human Language Technologies, Volume 1 (Long Papers), pp. 809–819. Association for Computational Linguistics, New Orleans, Louisiana (2018). https://doi.org/10.18653/v1/N18-1074, https://www.aclweb.org/anthology/N18-1074

137. Thorne, J., Vlachos, A., Cocarascu, O., Christodoulopoulos, C., Mittal, A.: The fact extraction and verification (fever) shared task. arXiv preprint arXiv:1811.10971 (2018)

138. Thorne, J., Vlachos, A., Cocarascu, O., Christodoulopoulos, C., Mittal, A.: The fever2. 0 shared task. In: Proceedings of the Second Workshop on Fact Extraction and VERification (FEVER), pp. 1–6 (2019)

139. Uscinski, J.E., Butler, R.W.: The epistemology of fact checking. Crit. Rev. **25**(2), 162–180 (2013)

140. Vicario, M.D., Quattrociocchi, W., Scala, A., Zollo, F.: Polarization and fake news: early warning of potential misinformation targets. ACM Trans. Web (TWEB) **13**(2), 1–22 (2019)

141. Vlachos, A., Riedel, S.: Fact checking: task definition and dataset construction. In: Proceedings of the ACL 2014 Workshop on Language Technologies and Computational Social Science, pp. 18–22 (2014)

142. Vlachos, A., Riedel, S.: Identification and verification of simple claims about statistical properties. In: Proceedings of the 2015 Conference on Empirical Methods in Natural Language Processing, pp. 2596–2601. Association for Computational Linguistics, Lisbon, Portugal (2015). https://doi.org/10.18653/v1/D15-1312, https://www.aclweb.org/anthology/D15-1312

143. Volkova, S., Shaffer, K., Jang, J.Y., Hodas, N.: Separating facts from fiction: Linguistic models to classify suspicious and trusted news posts on twitter. In: Proceedings of the 55th annual meeting of the association for computational linguistics (volume 2: Short papers), pp. 647–653 (2017)

144. Volkova, S., Shaffer, K., Jang, J.Y., Hodas, N.: Separating facts from fiction: linguistic models to classify suspicious and trusted news posts on Twitter. In: Proceedings of the 55th Annual Meeting of the Association for Computational Linguistics (Volume 2: Short Papers), pp. 647–653. Association for Computational Linguistics, Vancouver, Canada (2017). https://doi.org/10.18653/v1/P17-2102, https://www.aclweb.org/anthology/P17-2102

145. Wadden, D., et al.: Fact or fiction: verifying scientific claims. arXiv preprint arXiv:2004.14974 (2020)

146. Wadden, D., et al.: Fact or fiction: verifying scientific claims. In: Proceedings of the 2020 Conference on Empirical Methods in Natural Language Processing (EMNLP), pp. 7534–7550. Association for Computational Linguistics (2020). https://doi.org/10.18653/v1/2020.emnlp-main.609, https://www.aclweb.org/anthology/2020.emnlp-main.609

147. Wang, J., Mao, H., Li, H.: FMFN: fine-grained multimodal fusion networks for fake news detection. Appl. Sci. **12**(3), 1093 (2022)

148. Wang, N.X.R., Mahajan, D., Danilevsky, M., Rosenthal, S.: SemEval-2021 task 9: fact verification and evidence finding for tabular data in scientific documents (SEM-TAB-FACTS). In: Palmer, A., Schneider, N., Schluter, N., Emerson, G., Herbelot, A., Zhu, X. (eds.) Proceedings of the 15th International Workshop on Semantic Evaluation, SemEval@ACL/IJCNLP 2021, Virtual Event / Bangkok, Thailand, 5–6 Aug. 2021, pp. 317–326. Association for Computational Linguistics (2021). https://doi.org/10.18653/v1/2021.semeval-1.39
149. Wang, W.Y.: "Liar, liar pants on fire": a new benchmark dataset for fake news detection. arXiv preprint arXiv:1705.00648 (2017)
150. Wang, W.Y.: "Liar, Liar Pants on Fire": A new benchmark dataset for fake news detection. In: Proceedings of the 55th Annual Meeting of the Association for Computational Linguistics (Volume 2: Short Papers), pp. 422–426. Association for Computational Linguistics, Vancouver, Canada (2017). https://doi.org/10.18653/v1/P17-2067, https://www.aclweb.org/anthology/P17-2067
151. Wang, Z., Shan, X., Yang, J.: N15news: a new dataset for multimodal news classification. arXiv preprint arXiv:2108.13327 (2021)
152. Wardle, C., Derakhshan, H.: Information disorder: toward an interdisciplinary framework for research and policymaking (2017)
153. Williams, A., Nangia, N., Bowman, S.R.: A broad-coverage challenge corpus for sentence understanding through inference. arXiv preprint arXiv:1704.05426 (2017)
154. Williams, E., Rodrigues, P., Novak, V.: Accenture at CheckThat! 2020: if you say so: post-hoc fact-checking of claims using transformer-based models. arXiv preprint arXiv:2009.02431 (2020)
155. Wu, L., Rao, Y., Yang, X., Wang, W., Nazir, A.: Evidence-aware hierarchical interactive attention networks for explainable claim verification. In: Proceedings of the Twenty-Ninth International Conference on International Joint Conferences on Artificial Intelligence, pp. 1388–1394 (2021)
156. Yang, X., Lyu, Y., Tian, T., Liu, Y., Liu, Y., Zhang, X.: Rumor detection on social media with graph structured adversarial learning. In: Proceedings of the Twenty-ninth International Conference on International Joint Conferences on Artificial Intelligence, pp. 1417–1423 (2021)
157. Zellers, R., et al.: Defending against neural fake news. In: Advances in Neural Information Processing Systems, vol. 32 (2019)
158. Zeng, X., Abumansour, A.S., Zubiaga, A.: Automated fact-checking: a survey. Lang. Linguist. Compass 15(10), e12438 (2021)
159. Zhang, J., Dong, B., Philip, S.Y.: FakeDetector: effective fake news detection with deep diffusive neural network. In: 2020 IEEE 36th International Conference on Data Engineering (ICDE), pp. 1826–1829. IEEE (2020)
160. Zhang, W., Deng, Y., Ma, J., Lam, W.: AnswerFact: fact checking in product question answering. In: Proceedings of the 2020 Conference on Empirical Methods in Natural Language Processing (EMNLP), pp. 2407–2417. Association for Computational Linguistics (2020). https://doi.org/10.18653/v1/2020.emnlp-main.188, https://www.aclweb.org/anthology/2020.emnlp-main.188
161. Zhang, Y., Ives, Z., Roth, D.: Evidence-based trustworthiness. In: Proceedings of the 57th Annual Meeting of the Association for Computational Linguistics, pp. 413–423 (2019)
162. Zhong, W., et al.: Reasoning over semantic-level graph for fact checking. arXiv preprint arXiv:1909.03745 (2019)
163. Zhou, X., Jain, A., Phoha, V.V., Zafarani, R.: Fake news early detection: a theory-driven model. Digit. Threats: Res. Pract. 1(2), 1–25 (2020)

164. Zhou, X., Mulay, A., Ferrara, E., Zafarani, R.: Recovery: a multimodal repository for COVID-19 news credibility research. In: Proceedings of the 29th ACM International Conference on Information & Knowledge Management, pp. 3205–3212 (2020)

165. Zubiaga, A., Aker, A., Bontcheva, K., Liakata, M., Procter, R.: Detection and resolution of rumours in social media: a survey. ACM Comput. Surv. (CSUR) 51(2), 1–36 (2018)

166. Zubiaga, A., Liakata, M., Procter, R., Wong Sak Hoi, G., Tolmie, P.: Analysing how people orient to and spread rumours in social media by looking at conversational threads. PloS one 11(3), e0150989 (2016)

167. Zuo, C., Karakas, A., Banerjee, R.: A hybrid recognition system for check-worthy claims using heuristics and supervised learning. In: CEUR Workshop Proceedings, vol. 2125 (2018)

Topic Detection and Tracking in Social Media Platforms

Riccardo Cantini[✉] and Fabrizio Marozzo

DIMES Department, University of Calabria, Rende, Italy
{rcantini,fmarozzo}@dimes.unical.it

Abstract. The large amount of information available on the Web can be effectively exploited in several domains, ranging from opinion mining to the analysis of human dynamics and behaviors. Specifically, it can be leveraged to keep up with the latest news around the world, although traditional keyword-based techniques make it difficult to understand what has been happening over an extended period of time. In fact, they do not provide any organization of the extracted information, which hinders the general understanding of a topic of interest. This issue can be overcome by leveraging a Topic Detection and Tracking (TDT) system, which allows detecting a set of topics of interest, following their evolution through time. This work proposes a TDT methodology, namely *length-weighted topic chain*, assessing its effectiveness over two real-world case studies, related to the 2016 United States presidential election and the Covid19 pandemic. Experimental results show the quality and meaningfulness of the identified chains, confirming the ability of our methodology to represent well the main topics underlying social media conversation as well as the relationships among them and their evolution through time.

Keywords: Topic Detection · Topic Tracking · Latent Dirichlet Allocation · Covid19 · USA Presidential Election · Social Media

1 Introduction

Every day, a huge amount of digital data are produced on the Web, effectively exploitable to extract information in several application domains, including opinion mining [5], emotion analysis [3], news gathering [18], information diffusion [2], and influence maximization [9]. For this purpose, frameworks and tools for efficient computing in distributed and high-performance infrastructures are used [4], as well as special analysis techniques, which in the case of social media are often based on hashtags, particular keywords with high semantic content [8].

Information extracted on social media can be leveraged to keep up with the latest news, even if it is difficult to understand what has been happening over an extended period of time [11]. Indeed, traditional keyword-based search techniques do not organize retrieved information, hindering the global understanding of a topic of interest. To address this problem, Topic Detection and

C. Comito and D. Talia (Eds.): PerSOM 2022, LNICST 494, pp. 41–56, 2023.
https://doi.org/10.1007/978-3-031-31469-8_3

Tracking (TDT) systems were developed, which provide automated techniques for organizing large amounts of news streams in a way that helps users quickly interpret and analyze relevant information over time [1].

This paper describes a Topic Detection and Tracking methodology, namely *length-weighted topic chain*, aimed at finding the main topics of discussion in a given corpus, tracking their evolution over time and detecting the relationships among them. It is based on the *topic chain* model proposed by Kim et al. [11], by introducing several changes and improvements. In particular, our methodology overcomes a resolution-based issue of the original approach, related to the joint use of static connection probabilities and a sliding time window of fixed size. Specifically, we removed the time window, introducing an exponential decay mechanism applied to the probability of topic connection, which is computed with respect to the length of the chain. This ensures that the connection probabilities do not go to zero instantaneously as the window size is exceeded, but they smoothly decrease as the length of the chain increases, allowing greater flexibility in the creation of the chains.

An extensive experimental evaluation was carried out on two real-world case studies, related to the 2016 United States presidential election and the Covid19 pandemic. Identified chains in both cases are quite meaningful and coherent, with no conflicting topics within the same chain. This last aspect is more evident in the first case study, characterized by the rivalry between Donald Trump and Hillary Clinton, in which almost all identified topics have a neat political polarization. The main contributions of this research are the following:

- A novel length-weighted topic chain model is proposed, aimed at finding the main topics of discussion, effectively tracking their evolution over time by discovering high-quality chains with low noise and high coherence.
- It addresses the resolution-based issue of topic chains by dynamically adjusting topic connection probability, which allows the identification of links at different probability levels, between topics at an arbitrary temporal distance.
- A precise and in-depth investigation is conducted on the main topics underlying the Twitter conversation about the 2016 US presidential election and the Covid19 pandemic.

The remainder of the paper is organized as follows. Section 2 discusses related work and the main concepts of TDT systems. Section 3 describes the topic chain model. Section 4 describes in detail the proposed methodology. Section 5 presents the case studies and Sect. 6 concludes the paper.

2 Related Work

The main objective of Topic Detection and Tracking (TDT) is to extract information about the topics of discussion and their evolution over time automatically (i.e., without human intervention), starting from flows of news in different formats (e.g., text and audio). The key concepts of TDT are the following [1]:

- *Event*: it is something that occurs at a precise time and place, triggered by a set of causes and followed by a set of consequences.
- *Activity*: represents groups of events with the same purpose, which occur at certain times and places.
- *Topic*: it is defined as a seminal event or activity, together with all closely related events and activities.
- *Story*: refers to a multimodal source of information, such as a newspaper article, radio, or television broadcast.

The main tasks of a TDT process are discussed below, together with the main approaches present in the state of the art for the implementation of such systems.

2.1 Main Tasks of a TDT Process

Story Segmentation. It represents the process by which a multimodal stream of input data is broken down into stories. The input can be either in the form of audio (*Broadcast Story Segmentation*) or text (*Text Story Segmentation*). Story segmentation represents one of the main tasks of the TDT process, as a correct splitting is crucial to identify and follow the different topics of discussion.

First Story Detection. The goal of this task is to recognize, within a flow of chronologically ordered stories, the first story that deals with a specific topic. In particular, when a new story is detected, the system decides whether it deals with a previously encountered topic or is inherent to a new topic. This task is therefore a form of online clustering, where a cluster is created if the news is not sufficiently similar to any other already seen by the system.

Topic Tracking. The goal of Topic Tracking is the identification of stories related to a specific topic, given a stream of input stories. In *Traditional Topic Tracking* a statistical approach is exploited in order to analyze the association between stories and connect them through knowledge of the specific domain. *Adaptive Topic Tracking*, instead, is a more refined technique that uses a probabilistic approach to determine the correlation between topics and stories, by progressively adapting the topic model [14].

Topic Detection. It aims to identify the topics discovered through first story detection, tracing them through topic tracking techniques. In particular, clusters composed of stories relating to the same topic are identified. The topic detection task can be divided into two sub-categories. The first *Retrospective topic detection* deals with the search for topics occurs retrospectively on a collection of stories, which are grouped into clusters on the basis of the treated topic. The second *On-line topic detection* calculates the clustering structure progressively, sequentially processing a stream of stories.

Story Link Detection. Its purpose is to determine whether two given documents deal with the same topic or not. In particular, this task is framed as a binary classification on the presence of a link between the two documents, and is based on pair-wise document similarity/divergence measures.

2.2 Main Approaches to the Realization of TDT Systems

This section describes the main techniques used to build TDT systems. The main approaches in the literature, described in this section, are based on the use of clustering techniques, semantic classes, and vector spaces. A further approach, based on topic modeling and the use of particular structures called topic chains, will be explored in Sect. 4 together with the proposed methodology.

Clustering-based. TDT techniques following this approach aim to identify a topic-based clustering structure that represents a significant grouping of the processed documents, generally represented within a vector space. In the following, we discuss the main clustering-based techniques present in the literature.

Agglomerative Hierarchical Clustering. The approach proposed by Trieschnigg et al. [15] aims to solve two typical problems of topic-based clustering structures. Firstly, a hierarchical approach allows capturing topics at different levels of granularity, obtaining different fine-grained topics in the same macro-topic. Secondly, in a hierarchical representation where document clusters are defined at different levels of granularity, stories can be assigned to multiple clusters. The relationships between clusters are expressed through an n-ary tree in which, as the depth increases, there are nodes relating to increasingly specific sub-topics, up to the leaves that represent the topics with the greatest granularity.

Single-Pass Clustering. This is a widely used approach, due to its simplicity, high efficiency, and low cost, which makes it suitable when processing a large amount of data on a large scale [13]. It is based on a clustering structure built incrementally, based on the processed documents. In particular, given a document, it is compared with all the clusters present and assigned to one of them if the similarity exceeds a certain threshold. Otherwise, it will locate within a new cluster, representative of a new topic. The main disadvantage of this approach is that the temporal distance between the document candidate to be part of a cluster and those already assigned to it is not considered in any way. This can lead to the *topic drifting* issue, which is the deviation from the original topic caused by a lowering of the purity of the identified clusters. To overcome this problem, an improved version of the Single Pass has been developed by Zhe et al. [17]. It exploits the concept of sliding time window and a double similarity threshold $(\theta_{class}, \theta_{cand})$, with $\theta_{class} > \theta_{cand}$. Specifically, if the similarity is greater than θ_{class}, the story is assigned to a specific cluster. Otherwise, a check is made on θ_{cand}, to determine weaker links to candidate topics, which are validated later within the time window. If by the end of the time window a strong similarity (greater than θ_{class}) between the story and the candidate topic is not measured, this story will constitute a new cluster.

Semantic-Based. This approach, proposed by Makkonen et al. [12], is based on the use of semantic classes, i.e. classes of terms with similar meaning (places, names, temporal expressions). In particular, the semantic content of a document is represented through the use of four classes described in the following.

- *Names*: express the subjects involved in an event.
- *Terms*: express the occurrence of an event (nouns, verbs, and adjectives).
- *Time expressions*: represent points mapped on a time axis.
- *Places*: indicate the places involved in the carrying out of an event.

To be inherent to the same event, two documents do not necessarily have to coincide in all four classes. As an example, if two documents coincide in the class of time expressions and places, they are likely discussing the same event. In addition, if we consider large geographical areas, such as continents, the similarity will be weaker than that calculated on more specific areas. Therefore, this approach allows performing class-based comparisons, through the use of three different techniques described below.

General Term Weight. This technique is based on the intuition that in short online news the event being talked about is immediately identifiable. This is exploited by introducing weights for each term calculated on the basis of its occurrences and their position within the document.

Temporal Similarity. This technique is based on the fact that news related to new events tend to be published in bursts. In particular, there is usually an initial news story followed by a group of news published shortly after. Thus, these techniques exploit the temporal information to weigh the value obtained from the calculation of similarity. Particularly, a decay factor is introduced which is proportional to the temporal distance between a news and the original one.

Spatial Similarity. This technique exploits a geographical ontology in order to measure the similarity of the spatial references present in the documents. In particular, a hierarchical structure is used, comprised of continents, regions, nations, regions and cities, which can be represented as an n-ary tree. To measure the similarity between two places, the paths that go from the root of the tree to those places are identified. Then, the ratio between the length of the common path and the sum of the total lengths of these paths is calculated.

3   A Topic Modeling Based Approach: Topic Chain

Besides the main algorithms for Topic Detection and Tracking, based on clustering and semantic classes, described in Sect. 2, there is a further approach that relies on probabilistic topic modeling [6] and a particular structure called *topic chain* [11]. A topic chain consists of a temporal organization of similar topics that appear within a specified interval of time, represented as a sliding window on a global time axis. There are different elements that make up a topic chain:

- *Long-term topic*: it consists of a general topic, present in social media conversation or online news over a long period of time, such as the discussion about Covid19 pandemic or the war in Afghanistan.
- *Temporary issue*: it is a specific topic, that is talked about for a short period of time. It can be related to sporadic events or a part of a broader topic. An example can be a manifestation, which is generally a sporadic event, often connected to a long-term topic or to a specific trend on social media.
- *Focus shift*: it is the change over time of the particular aspect of a long-term topic on which news about that topic is focused. As an example contagion-prevention rules and vaccination within the general topic of Covid19.

The methodology is based on the creation of topic chains, aimed at understanding how topics and issues emerge, evolve, and disappear within the analyzed news corpus. This is achieved by observing long- and short-term topics, along with the different topic shifts occurring in the corpus. In particular, the methodology is comprised of three main steps, described in the following.

3.1 Topic Discovery

In this step, the analyzed corpus of news is divided into several time slices and the main topics in each time slide are found. The topic discovery step is performed by using the Latent Dirichlet Allocation (LDA) [7], a widely used algorithm for probabilistic topic modeling. LDA models each document as a random mixture of latent topics, while each topic is a distribution of terms over a fixed-sized vocabulary. Specifically, given K latent topics underlying a corpus composed of M documents of N words each, the generative process works as follows:

- For each document $d_i, i = 1, \ldots, M$, a multinomial distribution θ_i over the K latent topics is randomly sampled from a Dirichlet distribution with parameter α.
- For each topic $z_k, k = 1, \ldots, K$, a multinomial distribution ϕ_k over the N words is randomly sampled from a Dirichlet distribution with parameter β.
- For each word position $j = 1, \ldots, N$ of the document d_i, a topic $z_{i,j}$ is sampled from θ_i.
- The j-th word of d_i (i.e. $w_{i,j}$) is generated by random sampling from the multinomial distribution $\phi_{z_{i,j}}$.

Summing up, the total probability of the model is obtained as:

$$P(W, Z, \theta, \phi; \alpha, \beta) = \prod_{k=1}^{K} P(\phi_k; \beta) \prod_{i=1}^{M} P(\theta_i; \alpha) \prod_{j=1}^{N} P(z_{i,j}|\theta_i) P(w_{i,j}|\phi_{z_{i,j}}) \quad (1)$$

The various distributions, such as the specific mixture of each document in the corpus, are not known a priori and have to be learned via statistical inference. In particular, different approaches were proposed to deal with this task, by approximating the posterior distribution, such as Variational Bayes [7] and Monte Carlo Markov Chain (MCMC) algorithms like Gibbs Sampling [10].

3.2   Choice of the Topic Similarity Measure

A topic can be treated as a multinomial distribution over the words of the corpus vocabulary, as a ranked list of words, or as a vector in which each word of the vocabulary is associated with that topic with a certain probability. This allows the use of several metrics to compute the similarity between topics, introduced in the following.

- *Cosine similarity*: it measures the similarity between two given n-dimensional vectors as the cosine of the angle between them.
- *Jaccard coefficient*: it defines the similarity of two sets of items as the cardinality of the intersection divided by the cardinality of the union.
- *Kendall's τ coefficient*: it is a non-parametric measure of the rank correlation between two sets of items.
- *Discounted cumulative gain (DCG)*: it measures the overall normalized relevance of a set of ranked items by penalizing highly relevant documents appearing at a low position in the ranking.
- *Kullback-Leibler divergence (KL)*: it measures the dissimilarity, in probabilistic terms, between two given distributions.
- *Jensen-Shannon divergence (JS)*: it is the symmetric version of the KL divergence between two given distributions, obtained as the average divergence from their mixture distribution.

The choice of the most suitable topic similarity measure is done by finding the measure that identifies the best associations between topics of two consecutive time windows. In particular, the LDA model is trained for the time windows t and $t+1$, finding two distinct sets of topics $\phi^t = \phi_1^t, \ldots, \phi_k^t$ and $\phi^{t+1} = \phi_1^{t+1}, \ldots, \phi_k^{t+1}$. Then the topic-wise similarity is computed for each pair ϕ_i^t, ϕ_j^{t+1}, finding the top five most similar pairs. Finally, for each pair in the top five, the topic ϕ_i^t is substituted to ϕ_j^{t+1} and the log-likelihood of the data at time t is computed. This process is repeated for each similarity measure, by finding the one that minimizes the negative log-likelihood. This measure will be the selected one, as it leads to the most meaningful substitutions thus obtaining the set of topics that best explain the corpus.

3.3   Topic Chains Construction

In this step, topic chains are built by identifying sequences of similar topics through time. The corpus is divided into a sequence of time slices by using a sliding window and the similarity between topics is computed by leveraging the similarity measure identified in the previous step. In particular, denoted as $\phi^t = \phi_1^t, \ldots, \phi_k^t$ the topic distribution at time t, the construction process proceeds as follows:

1. The topic distribution at the previous time $t-1$, i.e. $\phi^{t-1} = \phi_1^{t-1}, \ldots, \phi_k^{t-1}$ is found and the similarity between ϕ_i^t and each topic ϕ_j^{t-1} is computed.

2. For each pair ϕ_i^t, ϕ_j^{t-1} such that their similarity is greater than a threshold, a link between them is created and the process moves to the next topic ϕ_{i+1}^t.
3. If no link was created by comparing ϕ_i^t with the topics ϕ^{t-1}, a comparison is made with topics in ϕ^{t-2}.
4. This process is iterated backward, until at least one connection is found or the size of the time window is exceeded.

Note that if a divergence measure is directly used (see step 2), such as KL or JS divergence, the measured value between the two considered topics must be less than the threshold for a link to be created.

3.4   Chains Analysis and Interpretation

As a last step, the obtained chains are analyzed in order to find long-term topics such as politics and economics, and temporary issues related to specific events and topics that do not last for a long period of time. Furthermore, the different focus shifts in long-term topics are identified, by analyzing the use of named entities along the chain. Specifically, a named entity is a real-world object, such as a person, location, organization, or product, characterized by a proper name.

4   Proposed Methodology

The topic chain methodology, described in Sect. 3, is characterized by a tuning phase in which the value of the threshold and the dimension of the sliding time window are selected against a wide set of possible values. However, the joint optimization of these hyper-parameters can lead to some issues. In the following we provide an in-depth description of these issues, together with the weighted variant we propose to overcome them.

4.1   Main Limitations of the Original Approach

Let's assume that a divergence measure is used for computing topic similarity so that a connection between topics is created when the divergence is below the threshold. By increasing the threshold value, the connection probability also increases, as this allows the association of topics with greater divergence. The increase in connection probability generally leads to the creation of longer chains, but can also negatively impact the meaningfulness of the obtained chains. In particular, as the size of the chain increases, it can incorporate other small chains and singlet topics, with the risk of introducing noise, i.e. non relevant or even contradictory links. This negative effect, which causes a general decrease of coherence, can be partially avoided by finding a suitable size for the sliding time window. Specifically, this parameter limits the number of possible links that can be created, by allowing the comparison only with a small number of previous time slices. However, the main limitation of this approach is that a time window of fixed size does not allow the emergence of links between time slices at a distance greater than that imposed by the window size. In fact, in order to identify distant connections it is necessary to increase the window size, which again can lead to the presence of noisy connections. Another way to reduce the presence of noisy links could be lowering the threshold value, but this would lead to the loss of chains with a lower connection probability.

By summing up, the main limitation of the original methodology is that it is not able to detect links at different probability levels and at an arbitrary distance in time, due to the joint action of the threshold and window size. In particular:

- Connections between time slices distant from each other need a wide time window. Consequently, they may not be isolated but included in broader chains along with other noisy connections.
- Lowering the threshold to remove noisy connections can cause the loss of weaker links, which does not allow to find chains at a lower probability level.

This is a resolution-based issue that is also present in other application domains. As an example, a similar drawback characterizes the DBSCAN clustering algorithm, which is not able to detect a global structure composed of clusters at different density levels.

4.2 Proposed Solution: Length-Weighted Topic Chain

In order to overcome the issues discussed in Sect. 4.1, we propose a variant of the topic chain methodology, namely *length-weighted topic chain*, which introduces an exponential decay of connection probabilities. Exponential decay is a widely used mechanism, exploited in several application domains, especially in modeling natural phenomena, such as radioactive decay, the variation of atmospheric pressure, and enzyme-catalyzed reactions. For what concerns TDT techniques in the literature, an example is provided by Xu et al. [16], that used an exponential decay in computing the similarity between two topics, which decreases as the temporal distance between them increases.

In our solution, the decay is computed with respect to the length of the topic chain. In particular, we removed the limitations imposed by the time window size, potentially allowing connections between topics on the whole temporal axis. In this way, the connection probability does not go to zero instantaneously, when the fixed size of the window is exceeded, but decreases smoothly as the length of the chain increases. This effect is obtained by dynamically modifying the threshold in relation to the current length of the chain. This threshold specifies the cutting value for topic divergence: specifically, two topics are linked to each other within the chain if their divergence is not greater than the threshold. The exponential decrease of the threshold is controlled by the decay factor λ, which also affects the length of the chain: larger values of this constant cause a more rapid decrease of the threshold, which results in lower connection probabilities and shorter chains. Formally, let $\phi_i^t, \phi_j^{t'}$ be a pair of topics detected in two different time slices t and t' with $t > t'$, and let th_0 be the initial value of the threshold used to test if a link can be created between two given topics. This threshold undergoes an exponential decay based on the current length of the chain L, defined as the number of links present in the chain up to $\phi_j^{t'}$. Therefore, the current value of the threshold is computed as follows:

$$th_L = th_0 \cdot e^{-\lambda L} \tag{2}$$

Afterwards, a link between ϕ_i^t and $\phi_j^{t'}$ is created within the topic chain if:

$$div(\phi_i^t, \phi_j^{t'}) \leq th_L \tag{3}$$

The introduction of the exponential decay allows to overcome the issues of the original methodology, which is not able to detect connections at different probability levels between topics at an arbitrary temporal distance. Indeed, by eliminating the time window, we are able to connect topics even if they belong to time slices distant from each other, by controlling at the same time the length of the chain through the decrease of the connection probabilities. This allows the formation of links between topics located at any point within the global time axis, and avoids the introduction of noise in chains of excessive length. Specifically, as the length of the chain increases, topics in subsequent time slices encounter greater resistance in forming a connection, which leads to the continuation of the chain only if the link is significant enough to overcome this resistance. Otherwise, the process iterates backward trying to link that topic to another in an earlier time slice. In that case, the topic will be connected to a shorter chain which is thus forked into a new, separate one.

5 Case Studies

In this section, we discuss the extensive experimental evaluation carried out by applying the proposed methodology to two different case studies, concerning social media conversation on the Twitter platform. Specifically, the first case study relates to the 2016 US presidential election, characterized by the rivalry between Hillary Clinton and Donald Trump, while the second focuses on content posted by users during the Covid19 pandemic. In the following, we provide a detailed description of the hyper-parameter tuning phase, together with an in-depth analysis of the identified chains. In our experiment, each time slice coincides with an entire day, and we run the LDA algorithm with a number of latent topics to be discovered equal to 10. In addition, the discovered chains will be analyzed at two different levels of granularity, to better grasp the connections between discussion topics and the daily evolution of social media conversation:

- *Topic-level*: $\{\phi_i^t, \phi_j^{t'}, \ldots, \phi_z^{t''}\}$, i.e., fine-grained chains identified by the connection between topics, in which there exists a link between each topic and its predecessor in the chain.
- *Day-level*: $\{t, t', \ldots, t''\}$, i.e., coarse-grained chains in which two days t and t' are connected if there exists a link between two topics ϕ_i^t and $\phi_j^{t'}$ detected in those days.

5.1   The 2016 US Presidential Election

This corpus comprises about 2.5 million tweets, posted by $521,291$ users regarding the 2016 US elections, published from October 10 2016 to November 7 2016. The analysis has been performed on tweets published in the main US swing states (Colorado, Iowa, Florida, Ohio, Michigan, Pennsylvania, Wisconsin, New Hampshire, North Carolina, and Virginia), characterized by high political uncertainty. In this way we obtained a representative corpus balanced with respect to the political polarization of the contained posts (*pro-Clinton* or *pro-Trump*). Tweets were collected through the public Twitter API, by using a set of keywords related to the presidential election, such as *#votetrump*, *#maga*, *#voteblue*, and *#USAelection2016*. Then, collected tweets were preprocessed in order to make them suitable for the subsequent analysis steps, as described below.

- We lowercased the text of each tweet, filtering out URLs, emojis, punctuation, and stopwords.
- We normalized each word by replacing accented characters with regular ones and by performing lemmatization.
- Tweets in a language other than English were filtered out.
- The most frequent bigrams in the corpus were found and collapsed in a single word, such as *hillary_clinton, donald_trump. bernie_facts*.

Hyper-parameter Tuning. Here we describe how the different hyper-parameters needed by the methodology were tuned. Firstly, we determined the most suitable topic similarity/divergence measure. In particular, we followed the approach described in Sect. 3.2. As shown in Fig. 1(a), we found that the best measure, which minimizes negative log-likelihood, is the Jansen-Shannon divergence. Therefore, we used this measure throughout the whole experimental evaluation.

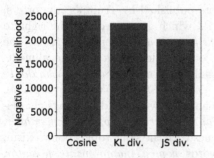

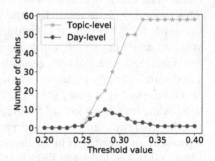

(a) Choice of the best similarity/divergence measure.

(b) Choice of the best threshold (cut value for JS divergence).

Fig. 1. Tuning of the main hyper-parameters of the methodology.

Once the divergence measure was chosen, we focused on the tuning of its cut value, i.e. the threshold used to test if two topics can be connected to create a new link within the chain. For this purpose, we plotted the number of topic-level and day-level chains, varying the threshold, as shown in Fig. 1(b). Two limit cases can be identified:

- If the cut value of the JS divergence is too low (below 0.24) no chain is detected, as this threshold results to be too strict.
- if the threshold is too high (above 0.35), all connections are merged in a single global day-level chain, as almost all subsequent days are connected by at least a pair of topics.

In order to ensure a trade-off between the number of chains at day and topic level, we selected a threshold value $th_0 = 0.28$. Indeed, this value shows a good ability in discriminating different trends evolving in subsequent days, causing at the same time the formation of a reasonable number of topic-level chains.

Discovered Chains. In the following we describe the most relevant chains identified by the proposed methodology, analyzing also the effects of the introduction of the exponential decay with a factor $\lambda = 0.05$. For a better understanding, chains are reported at day-level together with the general topic of discussion. Then the different connections between fine-grained topics are investigated, by providing various example tweets. Specifically, we found out what follows.

- *Sexism:* this chain connects 11, 12, 13, 15, and 16 October, and is characterized by a series of criticisms leveled at Donald Trump and its supporters. In particular, Trump was criticized for his sexually aggressive comments, which he justified by defining them *locker room talk*. This topic is characterized by the words *locker, room, talk*, and by the hashtag *#nevertrump*, which confirms the anti-trump polarity of the topic, which is constant throughout the entire chain. The chain continues with another anti-trump topic linked to sexism. This second topic is related to the tweets published by Trump's supporters, favorable to the repeal of amendment 19, which grants women the right to vote. As an example: *"Women are not fit for politics. #RepealThe19th"*. The publication of such content generated a lot of criticisms on Twitter, alimenting the anti-Trump discussion on the social platform: *"For anyone who thinks sexism doesn't exist and fighting for women's equality doesn't matter anymore: #repealthe19th is an actual hashtag"*. The main words and hashtags characterizing this topic are *women, #repealThe19, #nevertrump*, and *#imwithher*, a pro-Clinton hashtag. This chain continues with the same topic about sexism, identified in the following days by the words *women, inappropriate, predator*, and *#frankentrump*, a hashtag through which Trump was compared to Mary Shelley's Frankenstein in a derogatory way.
- *Disputes over the Clintons and elitism:* this chain covers the 17, 18, 22, 23, and 24 October, and is characterized by the discussion on Twitter about a series of disputes related to Hillary Clinton and her husband, the ex-president Bill Clinton. The first controversy is about Hillary Clinton's six-years tenure as a director of Walmart, and is characterized by words like *walmart, board,*

#corrupt, and *#podestamails*. Indeed, several emails were stolen from Hillary Clinton campaign chairman John Podesta's mail account, that document a close relationship between Clinton and Walmart. The chain continues with another topic about *elitism*, in which Hillary Clinton is accused of being supported by the American elite, pursuing the interests of a small circle of influential people. This topic is identified by the negative hashtag *#neverhillary* and the word *elite*, also used as a hashtag in tweets like the following: *"No doubt she has already been crowned queen by the US #elite"*. The last topic in this anti-Clinton chain relates to the controversies concerning the connection between Bill Clinton and Jeffrey Epstein, a millionaire accused of sexual abuse and child trafficking. In particular, conversation on social media focuses on Epstein's private island commonly referred to as Pedophile Island, and on the accusations made against the Clintons of having visited that place. Therefore, this topic is characterized by the words *pedophile*, *island*, *#lockherup*, and *#draintheswamp*, which are pro-Trump hashtags.

- *Trump's rhetoric:* this is a short chain linking 26 and 27 October, characterized by an anti-Trump topic. In particular, the republican candidate was criticized for his rhetoric, often considered violent, homophobic, and racist. Therefore, this topic is identified by the words *rhetoric*, *violent*, *trump*, and *#voteblue*, a hashtag in favor of Hillary Clinton.
- *Support from prominent public figures for Hillary Clinton:* this chain covers 28, 29 October, and 1, 2 November, days in which social media conversation focused on the support for the democratic candidate from public figures. As an example, Michelle Obama supported Hillary Clinton's candidacy by speaking at the rally held by Clinton on October 27 in Winston-Salem, North Carolina. Words and hashtags referring to this event are *women*, *rally*, *#imwithher*, and *#strongertogether*. Clinton also had the support of senator Jeanne Shaheen (*#senatorshaheen*, *#imwithher*) and the billionaire Richard Branson. In particular, the words *richard*, *branson*, *quote*, *trump*, refers to an interview released by Brandson in which the entrepreneur criticized Trump's violent temper, defining him as irrational and aggressive.
- *US elections and propaganda:* this is a short chain, covering 3 and 4 November, in which both pro-Clinton and pro-Trump supporters published content in favor of the two main candidates. Tweets are characterized by the main faction hashtags, such as *#maga* and *#votehillary*, and by hashtags encouraging people to vote, like *#vote*, *#vote2016* *#election2016*.

It is worth noting that the identified chains are quite meaningful and coherent from the viewpoint of political polarization. They also represent well the main topics underlying social media conversation, as well as the relationships among them and their evolution through time. Furthermore, we achieved these results thanks to the introduction of the exponential decay mechanism. Indeed, by using the traditional methodology, with a sliding time window of fixed size and a constant value for the threshold, we observed a degradation in the quality of the detected chains. As an example, the first chain about sexism is merged with the first part of the second chain, about Clinton and Walmart. Due to this, the first chain, characterized by anti-Trump themes, is polluted by a topic against Hillary Clinton. This introduces noise into the results due to an inversion of political polarization within the same chain. One way to avoid these noisy links could be to lower the cut value for JS divergence, but this would result in the loss of other links and small chains, such as the one referring to Trump's violent rhetoric.

5.2 Coronavirus Pandemic (Covid19)

This case study analyzes the tweets published in December 2020 related to the Covid19 pandemic. By applying the proposed methodology, we discovered five different chains, whose macro-topic is Covid19. These chains, which represent some of the aspects that the conversation on social media has focused on most, span the entire month under consideration, covering almost every day. This means that the identified chains do not present clear boundaries, contrary to those described in the previous case study. This is because these chains are not connected to specific events, but deal with the main topics on which the general discussion related to the pandemic is focused. Specifically, we found what follows:

- *General conversation about Covid19:* this chain connects topics that refer to Covid19 in a generic way, characterized by words like *global* and *covid*, and hashtags like *#covid19* and *#coronaviruspandemic*.
- *Anti-contagion protocols:* this chain connects a series of topics about the different protocols for contagion prevention, identified by trending hashtags on Twitter, such as *#washyourhands*, *#socialdistancing*, and *#wearamask*.
- *Remote job:* in this chain, the advantages of remote job are discussed, causing the presence of topics identified by words like *work* and *job* and hashtags like *#workfromhome* and *#remotejob*.
- *Vaccination and medical personnel:* this chain is characterized by published content regarding Covid19 vaccines, a topic identified by words and hashtags like *vaccine*, *#vaccine*, *#covidvaccine*. In addition, other hashtags like *#healthcare* and *#frontlineheroes* refer to healthcare workers and their vital contributions during the pandemic.
- *Christmas:* in this chain, the discussion on social media was about the effect of the pandemic on how people spent the Christmas holidays. The main words and hashtags are *christmas*, *#covidchristmas*, and *#christmas2020*.

6 Conclusions and Final Remarks

This paper describes a Topic Detection and Tracking methodology, namely *length-weighted topic chain*, aimed at finding the main topic of discussion in a given corpus, tracking their evolution over time, and detecting the relationships among them. The proposed methodology is based on the *topic chain* model and introduces an exponential decay mechanism applied to the probability of topic connection, which is computed with respect to the length of the topic chain. In this way, the main limitations of the original topic chain model can be overcome, allowing the identification of links at different probability levels, between topics located at any point within the global time axis, as well as an overall reduction of noise in the discovered chains.

The effectiveness of the proposed methodology was assessed over two real-world case studies, related to the 2016 United States presidential election and the Covid19 pandemic. Achieved results confirm the quality and meaningfulness of the identified chains, which represent well the main topics underlying social media conversation as well as their temporal evolution. Detected chains are also quite coherent, with no conflicting topics within the same chain, which is desirable in the case of politically-oriented news.

References

1. Allan, J.: Topic Detection and Tracking: Event-Based Information Organization, vol. 12. Springer, Heidelberg (2002). https://doi.org/10.1007/978-1-4615-0933-2
2. Arnaboldi, V., Contia, M.: Passarella, A., Dunbar, R.: Online social networks and information diffusion: the role of ego networks (2017). Preprint submitted to Elsevier, 8 November 2017
3. Belcastro, L., Branda, F., Cantini, R., Marozzo, F., Talia, D., Trunfio, P.: Analyzing voter behavior on social media during the 2020 us presidential election campaign. Soc. Netw. Anal. Min. **12**(1), 1–16 (2022)
4. Belcastro, L., Cantini, R., Marozzo, F., Orsino, A., Talia, D., Trunfio, P.: Programming big data analysis: principles and solutions. J. Big Data **9**(1), 1–50 (2022). https://doi.org/10.1186/s40537-021-00555-2
5. Belcastro, L., Cantini, R., Marozzo, F., Talia, D., Trunfio, P.: Learning political polarization on social media using neural networks. IEEE Access **8**, 47177–47187 (2020)
6. Blei, D.M., Lafferty, J.: Topic Models. Text Mining: Theory and Applications (2009)
7. Blei, D.M., Ng, A.Y., Jordan, M.I.: Latent Dirichlet allocation. J. Mach. Learn. Res. **3**(Jan), 993–1022 (2003)
8. Cantini, R., Marozzo, F., Bruno, G., Trunfio, P.: Learning sentence-to-hashtags semantic mapping for hashtag recommendation on microblogs. ACM Trans. Knowl. Discov. Data (TKDD) **16**(2), 1–26 (2021)
9. Cantini, R., Marozzo, F., Mazza, S., Talia, D., Trunfio, P.: A weighted artificial bee colony algorithm for influence maximization. Online Soc. Netw. Media **26**, 100167 (2021)
10. Griffiths, T.L., Steyvers, M.: Finding scientific topics. Proc. Natl. Acad. Sci. **101**(suppl_1), 5228–5235 (2004)
11. Kim, D., Oh, A.: Topic chains for understanding a news corpus. In: Gelbukh, A. (ed.) CICLing 2011. LNCS, vol. 6609, pp. 163–176. Springer, Heidelberg (2011). https://doi.org/10.1007/978-3-642-19437-5_13
12. Makkonen, J., et al.: Semantic classes in topic detection and tracking (2009)
13. Mohd, M., Crestani, F., Ruthven, I.: Construction of topics and clusters in topic detection and tracking tasks. In: 2011 International Conference on Semantic Technology and Information Retrieval, pp. 171–174. IEEE (2011)
14. Ren, X., Zhang, Y., Xue, X.: Adaptive topic tracking technique based on k-modes clustering. Comput. Eng. **35**(9), 222–224 (2009)

15. Trieschnigg, D., Kraaij, W.: TNO hierarchical topic detection report at TDT 2004. In: Topic Detection and Tracking Workshop Report (2004)
16. Xu, G., Meng, Y., Chen, Z., Qiu, X., Wang, C., Yao, H.: Research on topic detection and tracking for online news texts. IEEE Access **7**, 58407–58418 (2019)
17. Zhe, G., Zhe, J., Shoushan, L., Bin, T., Xinxin, N., Yang, X.: An adaptive topic tracking approach based on single-pass clustering with sliding time window. In: Proceedings of 2011 International Conference on Computer Science and Network Technology, vol. 2, pp. 1311–1314. IEEE (2011)
18. Zubiaga, A.: Mining social media for newsgathering: a review. Online Soc. Netw. Media **13**, 100049 (2019)

Fake News on Social Media: Current Research and Future Directions

Luciano Caroprese[1]([✉]), Carmela Comito[2], and Ester Zumpano[3]

[1] University G. D'Annunzio, Chieti-Pescara, Chieti, Italy
luciano.caroprese@unich.it
[2] Institute for High Performance Computing and Networking (ICAR), Rende, Italy
carmela.comito@icar.cnr.it
[3] DIMES, University of Calabria, Rende, Italy
e.zumpano@dimes.unical.it

Abstract. The escalation of false information related to the massive use of social media has became a challenging problem and great is the effort of the research community in providing effective solutions to detecting it. Fake news are spreading since decades, but with the rise of social media the nature of misinformation has evolved from text based modality to visual modalities, such as images, audio and video. Therefore, the identification of media-rich fake news requires an approach that exploits and effectively combines the information acquired from different multimodal categories. Multimodality is a key approach to improve fake news detection, but effective solutions supporting it are still poorly explored. More specifically, many different works exist that investigate if a text, an image or a video is fake or not, but effective research on a real multimodal setting, 'fusing' the different modalities with their different structure and dimension is still an open problem. The paper is a focused survey concerning a very specific topic that is the use of Deep Learning methods (DL) for multimodal fake news detection on social media.

Keywords: Fake News Detection · Multimodal · Social Media

1 Introduction

The world is highly connected and ideas easily spread in it. Moreover, the easy access to social media platforms has greatly increased so that offering the possibility to produce and share information, ideas and emotions in different forms such as text, video, audio, images. The freedom to share and access content without cost and supervision has surely positive implications, but it has also let to the consequent spread of low quality news and false news, referred to as fake news. Inaccurate and fake information is often intentionally posted online by malicious users in order to manipulate public emotions, influence people thoughts and actions, damage a group or a community, generate confusion and gain profits by misinformation.

C. Comito and D. Talia (Eds.): PerSOM 2022, LNICST 494, pp. 57–64, 2023.
https://doi.org/10.1007/978-3-031-31469-8_4

Fake news are misleading and difficult to catch by humans but also by AI algorithms, as often false information combines both fake and real information. The propagation of false information through social media has negative effects in many different aspects of social life.

The widespread diffusion of fake news on social media is a challenging problem. The research community is devoting great attention to the topic, putting in place important efforts to provide effective fake news detection solutions.

Early works on the fake news detection topic just rely on textual content. Anyhow, even if it is undoubted the necessity of analyzing news content in order to obtain a good indicator for detecting misinformation, it is clear that the only analysis of content is not sufficient. Post and online articles contain not only textual information but also audio, images and video, and misinformation can, therefore, spread through different modalities. Many different sophisticated tools exist to produce fake images or fake videos so that attracting users' attention and thus being shared.

Revealing a fake image involves an accurate analysis of the features related to the image, its associated caption, and the relationship between the image and the caption. Revealing a fake video implies, among others, a detailed analysis of the features related to the images, the sounds and the narrative associated to the video.

Thus far, besides textual information it is important to exploit and correctly combine information acquired from images and audios in order to detect fake news. Multimodality is the real key point to properly address the misinformation detection challenge. However, results obtained by the research community are not yet very effective. More specifically, many different works exist that investigate if a text, an image or a video is fake or not, but effective research on a real multimodal setting, 'fusing' the different modalities with their different structure and dimension, also including the news propagation network, is still an open problem. This paper surveys the recent literature covering various aspects of multimodality, like the news propagation network, text, image, audio, and discusses the fusion strategies proposed in the literature to merge the different modalities for fake news detection.

The proposal investigates and discusses an extensive collection of papers published in the recent years with the purpose of highlighting how deep learning can help fighting fake news. The paper is a focused survey exploring the specific topic of multimodal fake news detection with the lens of deep learning techniques. In fact, even if there are several useful surveys on fake news detection [7,14,15], only a few of them focus on multimodal strategies and even a smaller number of them is restricted to the use of deep leaning methods [1,2] and none of them relies on this topic in the social media domain. Therefore, the final purpose of this survey is to undertake a complete analysis of multimodal fake news detection by considering only the recent advancements in artificial intelligence brought by deep neural networks based solutions.

The paper is structured as follows. Section 2 presents a comprehensive overview of the literature, including models, methodologies, modality, data for fake news detection. Section 3 provides a discussion about the major challenges and opportunities, and traces future research directions. Section 3.2 concludes the survey.

2   Literature Review

In this section we review the works in the literature discussing models, methods and applications of deep learning techniques for multimodal fake news detection.

In particular, a detailed analysis of the selected papers is provided throughout the section. For each study in the literature, we extracted the most important features like the method implemented, the data type and size used, the evaluation methods adopted, the accuracy for each method, the results achieved.

[16] proposed SpotFake, a multimodal framework for fake news detection, exploiting both the textual and visual features of an article. Specifically, BERT is used to learn text features, while image features are learned from a CNN, VGG19 pre-trained on ImageNet dataset. All the experiments were performed on two publicly available datasets, MediaEval and Weibo A. Authors stated that the proposed model performs better than the current state-of-the-art.

[2] exploited that accepts an article's text and image as inputs. After that, a single vector is created by concatenating the outputs. Experimental validation has been carried out on the Fakeddit dataset, using both unimodal and multimodal solutions. According to experiments, the multimodal technique had an accuracy of 87% and produced the best outcomes.

[11] proposed the EM-FEND framework that is based on the extraction of visual entities to understand the semantics of images. To this purpose the authors considered a variety of data modality: text, OCR text, news-related high level semantics of images e.g., celebrities and landmarks, visual CNN features of the image, the embedded text in images. The different features are then concatenated by considering among others, correlations between text and images and inconsistency. Authors claimed that extensive experiments show their model outperforms the state of the art.

[20] proposed a Similarity-Aware FakE news detection method (SAFE) which exploit multimodal data, more exactly the textual and visual features from news. To this purpose, neural networks are used to extract the textual and visual features, also deriving a similarity among them. The aim of the approach is to classify a news by using either its text or images, or the mismatch between the text and images. Experiments have been performed on large-scale real-world data (PolitiFact, GossipCop), showing the effectiveness of the proposed method.

In the paper of [19] is proposed the Multimodal Consistency Neural Network (MCNN) tool, which is composed of five modules: the textual feature extraction that exploit BERT, the visual semantic feature extraction, the visual tampering feature extraction, the similarity measurement, and the multimodal fusion module. The visual tampering feature extraction focuses on physical levels feature extraction such as malicious image tampering and recompression by usiNg ResNet. The key aspect of the approach is THE similarity measurement module that evaluates the correlation between the text information and the visual one. The different features are then fused by means of attention mechanisms. The framework has been evaluated over 4 Twitter datasets, MCG-FNeWS, Politi-Fact, MediaEval, Yang dataset, showing promising results.

[17] proposed a multimodal fake news detection model exploiting text, comments and images and based on word embedding and convolutional neural network (VGG-19). Precisely, the model is composed of the following components: (1) input embedding layer to obtain word embedding and image embedding; (2) Cross-modal Attention Residual (CARN) layer to reinforce the target modality feature representation by selectively extracting information from another source modality; (3) self-attention residual network layer to capture the interactions between different sequence element pairs and transmit original textual information to MCN; (4) By simultaneously extracting textual feature representation from the original and fused textual data, the Multichannel Convolutional Neural Network (MCN) can reduce the impact of noisy information that may be produced by the crossmodal fusion component. (5) fake news detection module. Experiments have been performed on four real-world datasets: MediaEval, Weibo A, Weibo B. The model exceeds cutting-edge techniques, according to the results, and learns more discriminable feature representations.

[12] makes use of network, textual, and relaying elements like hashtags and URLs and categorizes articles by concatenating the embeddings of the features. Textual features are obtained by using word embedding to represent each word by a low dimensional vector and input this to an LSTM to find the contextual embedding of each tweet. As relaying features are considered five tweet-level features, including hashtag count, URL count, retweet count, mention count and favorite count. For what concerns network features, the framework constructs a network that captures the interactions between users and tweets, creating this way a directed graph of user mentions such that each tweet is connected to a user if their name is mentioned in the tweet text. Using this graph, authors created a one-hot vector of user mentions per tweet. The framework has been evaluated over two datasets, PHEME and Volkova dataset. Results shown that the approach is comparable with state-of-the-art performance.

[13] propose Shared Cross Attention Transformer Encoders (SCATE), a new idea that uses shared layers and cross-modal attention to encode both text and image information using deep convolutional neural networks and transformer-based techniques. Through attentional mechanisms, SCATE integrates the many modalities by focusing on the crucial components of each in relation to the others. A detailed experimental evaluation has been carried out over both Twitter and Weibo datasets like MediaEval, Weibo A, Weibo B.

[8] propose the Attention based Multimodal Factorized Bilinear (AMFB) framework to detect multimodal fake news. The framework has been designed with the intention to reveal the maximum correlation between visual and textual information. This framework has four different sub-modules: i) Attention Based Stacked Bidirectional Long Short Term Memory (ABSBiLSTM) for textual feature representation, ii) Attention Based Multilevel Convolutional Neural

Network-Recurrent Neural Network (ABM-CNN-RNN) for visual feature extraction, iii) multimodal Factorized Bilinear Pooling (MFB) attention mechanism for feature fusion and finally iv) Multi-Layer Perceptron (MLP) for the classification. Experimental results performed on two real-world dataset, MediaEval and Weibo A, shown the effectiveness of the approach.

[4] proposed the TRANSFAKE framework that considers different modalities like news content, comments and images for fake news detection. The textual features are extracted with BERT while for the visual one is used a Faster-RCNN model. TRANSFAKE fuses the different features with a Transformer-based model. It employs multiple tasks, i.e. rumor score prediction and event classification, as intermediate tasks for extracting useful hidden relationships across various modalities. These intermediate tasks promote each other and encourage TRANSFAKE making the right decision. Extensive experiments on three real-life datasets (PolitiFact, GossipCop, Weibo A) demonstrate that TRANSFAKE outperforms state-of-the-art methods.

[9] proposed the GCAN framework, Graph-aware Co-Attention Networks whose main aim is to enable explainable fake news detection on social media. After employing a dual co-attention approach to capture the correlations between user interaction/propagation and tweet's content, Lu et al. concatenate models of user interaction, word representations, and features related to the propagation. To learn the representation of retweet propagation based on user attributes, authors used convolutional and recurrent neural networks. In order to learn the graph-aware representation of user interactions, a graph convolution network is employed to model the potential interactions between users. Both the co-influence of the source tweet and user engagement, as well as the relationship between the source tweet and retweet propagation, can be learned using the dual co-attention mechanism. The binary forecast is produced using the learned embeddings. The framework has been evaluated on a real-world dataset, the Ma dataset [10]. The outcomes shown that the novel approach could be successfully applied for fake news detection by exploiting the propagation network.

[3] propose an interesting multimodal multi-image system in order to perform a binary classification of on line articles by combining textual, visual and semantic information; moreover, differently from other approaches, in the case of an article in which more that an image is present, it extracts and combines features extracted from all of them. BERT is used to obtain textual features, whereas to a obtain visual characteristics a VGG-19 model, an LSTM layer, and a mean pooling layer are employed.

In terms of semantic representation, it refers to the correspondence between text and image that is obtained applying the cosine similarity between the image tags embeddings and the title, this last is a type of information that is rarely considered in fake news detection. Experimentation is performed using the FakeNewsNet collection. More in details, from the GossipCop posts of such collection authors collects 2,745 fake news and 2,714 real news. The proposed multimodal multi-image system outperforms the BERT baseline by 4.19% and SpotFake by 5.39% and achieves an F1-score of 79.55%.

[5] propose a binary classification of fake news called DeepNet. DeepNet is modeled as a deep neural network that performs its task by considering not only the content of the news shared on social media but also exploits the relationship the user exhibits in the social network. The proposal is built considering the tensor factorization method, therefore a tensor is in charge of expressing the social context of news articles as combination of different information related to the news itself, the user, and group with whom the user interacts. DeepNet is structured as follows: it presents one embedding layer, three convolutional layers, one LSTM layer, seven dense layers, moreover it uses ReLU for activation and the softmax function to perform the binary classification. DeepNet is tested on the following datasets: Fakeddit and BuzzFeed (Kaggle, a). This last contains news from articles obtained related to U.S. election in a temporal interval of a week and labeled as either true news or fake news. The binary classification accuracy for the Fakeddit dataset is 86.4 %, and the accuracy for the BuzzFeed dataset is 95.2%.

[6] use four different modalities to perform binary classification of fake news over the Fakeddit dataset: the news' text content, related comments, photos, and any remaining metadata from other modalities. The proposed architecture allows to aggregate these modalities at different levels and considering different data fusion methods. The best result shows an accuracy of 95.5% and has been obtained by separately pre-training each modality, and then training only the fusion and classification layers on top.

[18] propose SERN, the Stance Extraction and Reasoning Network that allows to associate, given a post, its stances representations that are implied in the reply associated to the post itself. Text and images are considered into the proposal and a multimodal representation of these features is performed in order to binary classify fake news. The method works as follows: given a post containing multimodal news, an extractor first construct stances, i.e. post-reply pairs. Then, BERT is used to extract textual features and a pretrained ResNet-152 is used to retrieve visual features. Textual and visual features are therefore concatenated so that obtaining a multimodal feature representation. This last is then the input of a Multi-Layer Perceptron (MLP) that is in charge of performing a binary classification of the post. Experimentation demonstrates the proposal outperforms the state-of-the art baselines on two public datasets: PHEME dataset and a reduced version of the Fakeddit dataset created by the authors. Results show an accuracy of 96.63 % for Fakeddit and of 76.53% on PHEME.

3   Discussion

3.1   Major Challenges in Multimodal Fake News Detection

Fake news affect both online and offline social communities and different proposals exist in the recent literature investigating at different levels and with different strategies the problem. Multimodal approaches for fake news detection have been proved to be a viable effective approach to address disinformation, however, many are still the challenges that remain to be addressed.

- **Datasets:** Different multimodal datasets exist, but they often are related to two or few modalities such as text and images. These datasets have generally small size, expose content in just one language, and often are imbalanced either in the fake or real news. An additional issue is that in order to cope with different styles and different topics, datasets from heterogeneous platforms should be available. Therefore, urgent is the need of real and complete multimodal datasets containing different modalities such as text, images, video audio, social content, temporal and network propagation features.
- **Finer classification:** Existing fake news detection models are mainly binary classifiers that determine whether a piece of news is false or not. This strategy is often not sufficient and a multi-class classification or even a regression task should be used. The final aim should allow to enable prioritized reasoning and consequent strategies in the presence of fake news detection.
- **Scalability:** Since deep neural networks are complex and costly to build, and as most existing multimodal models use multiple deep neural networks (one per modality), they are not scalable as the number of modalities grows. Furthermore, many existing models require extensive computing resources, including large amounts of memory storage and processing units. As a result, when developing new architectures, the scalability of proposed models should be considered.

3.2   Conclusion

The paper provided a rigorous and in-depth survey on a very specific topic related to the use of deep learning for multimodal fake news detection on social media. The paper analyzed a large number of deep learning approaches and provided, for each work surveyed, an analysis of the rational behind the approach, highlighting some relevant features such as the DL method used, the type of data analyzed, the datasets used, the fusion strategy adopted and the eventual domain-invariant features.

Acknowledgments. This work was partially supported by project SERICS (PE00000014) under the NRRP MUR program funded by the EU - NGEU.

References

1. Alam, F., et al.: A survey on multimodal disinformation detection (2021). https://doi.org/10.48550/ARXIV.2103.12541, https://arxiv.org/abs/2103.12541
2. Alonso-Bartolome, S., Segura-Bedmar, I.: Multimodal fake news detection (2021). https://doi.org/10.48550/ARXIV.2112.04831
3. Giachanou, A., Zhang, G., Rosso, P.: Multimodal multi-image fake news detection. In: 2020 IEEE 7th International Conference on Data Science and Advanced Analytics (DSAA), pp. 647–654 (2020). https://doi.org/10.1109/DSAA49011.2020.00091

4. Jing, Q., Yao, D., Fan, X., Wang, B., Tan, H., Bu, X., Bi, J.: TRANSFAKE: multi-task transformer for multimodal enhanced fake news detection. In: 2021 International Joint Conference on Neural Networks (IJCNN), pp. 1–8 (2021)

5. Kaliyar, R.K., Kumar, P., Kumar, M., Narkhede, M., Namboodiri, S., Mishra, S.: DeepNet: an efficient neural network for fake news detection using news-user engagements. In: 2020 5th International Conference on Computing, Communication and Security (ICCCS), pp. 1–6 (2020). https://doi.org/10.1109/ICCCS49678.2020.9277353

6. Kirchknopf, A., Slijepčević, D., Zeppelzauer, M.: Multimodal detection of information disorder from social media. In: 2021 International Conference on Content-Based Multimedia Indexing (CBMI), pp. 1–4 (2021). https://doi.org/10.1109/CBMI50038.2021.9461898

7. Kumar, S., Shah, N.: False information on web and social media: a survey (2018). https://doi.org/10.48550/ARXIV.1804.08559, https://arxiv.org/abs/1804.08559

8. Kumari, R., Ekbal, A.: AMFB: attention based multimodal factorized bilinear pooling for multimodal fake news detection. Expert Syst. Appl. **184**, 115412 (2021)

9. Lu, Y.J., Li, C.T.: GCAN: graph-aware co-attention networks for explainable fake news detection on social media. In: Proceedings of the 58th Annual Meeting of the Association for Computational Linguistics, pp. 505–514 (2020)

10. Ma, J., Gao, W., Mitra, P., Kwon, S., Jansen, B.J., Wong, K.F., Cha, M.: Detecting rumors from microblogs with recurrent neural networks, IJCAI 2016, pp. 3818–3824 (2016)

11. Qi, P., et al.: Improving fake news detection by using an entity-enhanced framework to fuse diverse multimodal clues, pp. 1212–1220 (2021)

12. Rezayi, S., Soleymani, S., Arabnia, H.R., Li, S.: Socially aware multimodal deep neural networks for fake news classification. In: 2021 IEEE 4th International Conference on Multimedia Information Processing and Retrieval (MIPR), pp. 253–259 (2021). https://doi.org/10.1109/MIPR51284.2021.00048

13. Sachan, T., Pinnaparaju, N., Gupta, M., Varma, V.: SCATE: shared cross attention transformer encoders for multimodal fake news detection. In: Proceedings of the 2021 IEEE/ACM International Conference on Advances in Social Networks Analysis and Mining, ASONAM 2021, pp. 399–406 (2021)

14. Shu, K., Sliva, A., Wang, S., Tang, J., Liu, H.: Fake news detection on social media: a data mining perspective. SIGKDD Explor. Newsl. **19**(1), 22–36 (2017)

15. da Silva, F.C.D., Vieira, R., Garcia, A.C.B.: Can machines learn to detect fake news? A survey focused on social media. In: HICSS (2019)

16. Singhal, S., Dhawan, M., Shah, R.R., Kumaraguru, P.: Inter-modality discordance for multimodal fake news detection. In: MMAsia 2021 (2021)

17. Song, C., Ning, N., Zhang, Y., Wu, B.: A multimodal fake news detection model based on crossmodal attention residual and multichannel convolutional neural networks. Inf. Process. Manage. **58**(1), 102437 (2021)

18. Xie, J., Liu, S., Liu, R., Zhang, Y., Zhu, Y.: SERN: stance extraction and reasoning network for fake news detection. In: ICASSP 2021 - 2021 IEEE International Conference on Acoustics, Speech and Signal Processing (ICASSP), pp. 2520–2524 (2021). https://doi.org/10.1109/ICASSP39728.2021.9414787

19. Xue, J., Wang, Y., Tian, Y., Li, Y., Shi, L., Wei, L.: Detecting fake news by exploring the consistency of multimodal data. Inf. Process. Manag. **58**(5), 102610 (2021)

20. Zhou, X., Wu, J., Zafarani, R.: SAFE: similarity-aware multi-modal fake news detection (2020). https://doi.org/10.48550/ARXIV.2003.04981, https://arxiv.org/abs/2003.04981

Incivility Balanced? Civil vs. Uncivil Speech in Online Political Discussions as Dependent on Political Parallelism

Daniil Volkovskii[1,2]($\boxtimes$) and Svetlana Bodrunova[3]

[1] National Research University Higher School of Economics, Moscow, Russia
dvolkovskiy@hse.ru
[2] ITMO University, Saint Petersburg, Russia
[3] Saint-Petersburg State University, Saint Petersburg, Russia
s.bodrunova@spbu.ru

Abstract. This paper explores the balance between civility and incivility in Russian online political discussions in their relation to platform-based political parallelism. So far, the deliberative quality of communication on online forums and social networks has been seen as dependent on discussion structure, contextual factors, user traits and intentions, and textual features of the discussions, especially negative ones like incivility. However, of the latter, interdependence of (in)civility patterns and political parallelism of media where the discussions take place have not been explored well. Moreover, while incivility is studied extensively, its balancing practice, namely explicit civility and respect, usually escapes scholarly attention. In Russia, political discussions, media, and even platforms demonstrate strong political polarization, forming a peculiar picture of political parallelism. Polarization fuels political hostility that may have civil and uncivil patterns influencing the way of networked talk. To explore to what extent political positioning of the discussion milieus, e.g., media / media accounts where discussions take place, alters the volume and the nature of political (in)civility, we explore two cases, the first used as a baseline one and the second as the target one. For this, we use discourse analysis and descriptive statistics to show that incivility in the Russian-language online discussions is partly compensated by explicit civility, while remaining dominant in the fabric of political discussions. Moreover, we show the difference in the volume and nature of (in)civility within the comment sections of oppositional and pro-state media. Our results suggest hint to the 'free speech vs. hate speech' dilemma, as the comments in the oppositional media appear to be more hostile, while those on the pro-state accounts look less polluted by aggression.

Keywords: Online Deliberation · Networked Discussions · Political Conversation · Incivility · Russia · Platform Affordances · Political Parallelism

1 Introduction

The recent research on dissonant publics [1] and cumulative deliberation [2–4] allows for interpreting communication on social media and digital forums as a form of online deliberation dependent on features of networked discussion structure, cultural factors, and user traits and intentions. The normative theory of the political communication process claims that political discussions of deliberative nature are open, polite, and respectful, and are intended for mutual understanding [5–7]. In fact, there is a vast number of studies dedicated to such a central category in a political dialogue as civility [8–11]. However, when analyzing political Internet conversations in practice, a contradiction can be observed, since only a minority of political discussions characterized by considerable opinion polarity, are civil, polite, respectful of the audience. While online media allow citizens to freely discuss political issues and have the potential to facilitate political talk, not all online comments contribute to achieving this ideal [12–14]. An extensive body of research reveals that the prevalence of rude and intolerant communication (insults, stereotypes, or hatred) in Internet milieus can complicate the processes of deliberative discussions and reaching consensus in them [15–18].

Despite the growth in the number of studies on civility, there is not much knowledge on whether and how exactly (un)civil user behavior in comment sections is linked to the political stance of media. Most research in this area is done with a focus on for Western social mediated discussions, while such studies are still rare for countries with less stable democratic traditions.

In terms of uncivil speech online, the Russian-speaking Internet segment represents a special but telling case. First, offensive speech has centuries ago formed a sub-language called *mat* [19], which has passed through massive de-tabooing in the recent decades [20]. Second, online speech on Russian-speaking platforms has been demonstrating growth of radicalization and aggressivity since at least as early as the late 2000s [21], while Internet speech remained more free and much less regulated than that of offline media throughout the 2000s and 2010s [22]. Third, the rapid socio-economic and political changes of the 1990s has polarized the society not only politically but also in assessment of the Soviet and recent post-Soviet past, and politicized speech has brought to life multiple political pejoratives that serve for demarcation of individual and groups along the lines of historic memory [23]. Thus, the dilemma of 'hate speech vs. free speech' [24] for Russia has gained peculiar forms, highly relevant, though, for most other post-Soviet states and may, due to intensity of use of offensive speech, help discover and generalize the linkages between incivility in online discussions and their other structural or content parameters.

Thus, it is not surprising that, as previous research on Russian networked discussions shows, incivility plays a significant role in mass-scale online political discussions, becoming a key marker of strong opinion polarization [25] which fuels political hostility, and vice versa. At the same time, political hate speech may perform constructive functions within a heated political discussion, including spurring discussion dynamics, 'us – them' recognition, and contextualization of mutual pretentions [23]. What we have also shown earlier, though, is that uncivil speech tends to diminish when users discuss substantial issues, while growing in single non-dialogical comments or aggressive phatic communication, especially when users label each other as bots or trolls [25]. In this paper, we extend our exploration of uncivil political speech to possibilities of balancing it with explicit civility in discussions.

Moreover, we expect that the political stance of media affects the levels of incivility in user commenting. This is why we explore counter-balancing incivility by explicit civility in user comments on media accounts of politically polar media, thus aiming at detecting political parallelism expressed via (un)civil speech. Political parallelism has been explored for effects in traditional media [26, 27], but it remains practically unexplored for platforms or media portals/accounts as communicative milieus, especially in terms of incivility studies.

To tackle these issues, we study the recent polarized discussions on two topics, namely the pension system reform and the court sentence to the non-systemic political activist Alexei Navalny, in terms of (in)civility of public dialogue. The cases have been selected by the principle of maximum dissimilarity. The pension reform case has been explored on VK.com, as this platform is known as less politicized, more populated by 'average citizens', and less a political filter bubble than the Russian-speaking segments of Facebook [28], Twitter [29], or YouTube [30]. Thus, this case works for us as a baseline one that allows to assess (in)civility on politically polar comment sections and see whether the online hostility has grown much from 2018 to 2021. The target case is that of Alexey Navalny's sentencing, as this case was one of the most polarizing, was accompanied by street protest, and directly marked the socio-political cleavages in the Russian society. Unlike many other events related to political opposition, this case was intensely covered by both oppositional and pro-state media and commented on their websites and in their accounts on social media, which makes this case suitable for studies of political parallelism in (in)civility.

We use discourse analysis and descriptive statistics in our study, as they help investigate the volume and nature of civil and uncivil patterns of online political talk. The approach to discourse analysis of uncivil speech is developed by Misnikov [31] based on the works on deliberative democracy by Jürgen Habermas. The scholar has summarized and offered a range of discursive aspects of online discussions, including activity, interactivity, civility, rationality, argumentation, dialogicity, and presence of basic validity claims, as formulated by Habermas. In Misnikov's method, these variables independently guide coding of user texts for assessment of their deliberative quality (see an example in [31] and [32]). We have applied his approach to 14 discussion threads that contained 6.347 comments published on VK.com and analyzed in terms of types of in(civility).

However, the method developed by Misnikov (who follows Habermas quite closely in assessing the discursive features and not assessing the discussion context) implies that the core of potential consensus lies only in the texts themselves; no external factors are assessed. Coming from media studies, though, we believe that external factors may also shape the emergent consensus – or, at least, move the scales of the emergent majority's opinion to this or that side in the process of cumulative deliberation [3]. In our earlier studies, we have divided contextual factors that may shape discussion content into the context of a discussion and the context beyond the discussion, according to the current critical discourse theory and studies of online semiotics [33]. The context beyond a discussion comprises factors that may shape the structure of consensus and the process of reaching it. In this paper, we check the relations between political bias of the media that post news and the civility of the comments that gather under their posts, thus checking whether political parallelism of legacy media present online is a meaningful factor in shaping the cumulative patterns of opinion formation.

Also, the novelty of our paper lies in the fact that both cases, the pension reform and the court verdict to Navalny, have got (somewhat understandably, given the circumstances) little attention from Russian scholars, while they have been one of the most actively discussed and certainly polarized the Russian public sphere.

The remainder of the paper is organized as follows. Section 2 provides a review of theoretical works on public deliberation vs. uncivil speech online. Section 3 formalizes the research questions and hypotheses. Section 4 describes the methods and sampling, while Sect. 5 provides the results according to the RQs. Section 6 concludes the paper by discussing the results and putting them in context.

2 Theoretical Background

2.1 Civility and Incivility as Concepts. The Approach to Analyzing Them in Online Speech

This research is based on the deliberative theory by Jürgen Habermas. This approach plays a huge role in deliberative studies. The deliberative model of democracy proposed by the German philosopher is based on continuous and maximally broad political discourse in society the results of which are determined by the power of arguments and conditioned by normativity of participation modes [34]. The concept implies that true problems of society, directions of their solution, and optimal ways to achieve goals are identified in the course of collective reflection.

The concept of democratic deliberation implies a purposeful, respectful, civil discussion where both ordinary citizens and representatives of institutions reach consensus in a deliberative way and make decisions. As it is the normative conditions of argumentation that critically define the quality of deliberation, civility of the communicative process within societal deliberative efforts inevitably becomes one of the key concepts in the normative tradition of political deliberation studies [35–38]. However, the concept of civility still lacks conceptual clarity across disciplines, as it is investigated by scholars from political science, communication, sociology, and other fields. Hence, there is no clear definition of civility. Some scholars understand civility as politeness, etiquette, or manners [39–41], some compare it to forgiveness [35], others to respect for persons [42, 43]. One area where the literature agrees is that politeness or mutual respect is a necessary and, for some, sufficient part of any definition of civility [17, 44–46]. Nevertheless, various meanings of mutual respect and politeness across cultures [47] make it more complicated to define civility. There are also concerns that overemphasis on politeness might inhibit the free flow of ideas in political conversation, resulting in a very polite, restrained, and barely human discourse [11]. Thus, civility is described as a central component of deliberation that presupposes respect for and affirmation of all people and their opinions, even if there is a contention [48].

The same problem may be when it comes to conceptualizing incivility. Interestingly, incivility is not defined as 'lack of civility' but as a separate, self-sustaining, and active form of communication, with a plethora of considerable options in various works. Verbal incivility can be determined as a set of verbal behaviors (both oral and written) that threaten not only interpersonal relations between interrogators but also the democratic quality of public discourse [11, 49, 50]. Verbal incivility frequently includes threatening and aggression, intimidation, disrespectful speech, hostility and hate speech. Some works, though, still insist that incivility in its milder forms is the lack of respect for others and their ideas.

Coe et al. indicate one more aspect of defining incivility [18] which can be observed in comments involving rude naming, lying, vulgarity, aspersion, or usage of pejoratives. Thus, studies of incivility often conflate inherently harmful behaviors (such as expressions of racism, sexism, or hate speech) with expressions that, while disrespectful, vulgar, harsh, are not necessarily offensive [16–18, 51, 52].

Furthermore, scholars have examined the implications of civil and uncivil political discourse online. For example, previous research has shown that exposure to online incivility fosters political polarization [53, 54], promotes further use of incivility [55, 56], and decreases willingness to read others' comments online [54]. Uncivil comments that unnecessarily disrespect, label, and attack others derail the focus of a discussion and undermine citizen engagement [5, 57, 58], while reason-based opinion exchanges online can facilitate deliberation and active political engagement [56]. However, differences are inherent in political sphere and are not necessarily harmful to the democratic process. Our previous research suggests that political offense in polarized speech has positive functions, including fueling the discussions, mutual recognition of users with similar views, opinion cumulation, and contextualization of opinion via the use of historic metaphors and memories [23]. Moreover, aggressive speech demarcates non-substantial and aggressive phatic communication from substantial discussion [25]. The theory of cumulative deliberation implies that users have a right for expressing emotions, including negative and even aggressive emotions if such emotions do not surpass legal limits or strong conventional borders of civil speech. This means that incivility must be studied very attentively, to distinguish negative but legitimate emotions from conventionally illegitimate, unlawful, or propagandistic practices.

In this paper, though, we will use the broadest possible definition of civility and incivility, as there are still no conventionally shared academic approaches or instruments to distinguish between legitimate and illegitimate uncivil speech in online discussions. For this, we have selected the approach developed by Yu. Misnikov [31]. Civility is used to characterize the qualitative nature of a public online discussion and understood as demonstrating a tolerant attitude towards a discussion participant, his/her position, and/or the object of discussion. Consequently, incivility means an intolerant attitude towards a participant, his/her position, and/or the object of discussion.

2.2 (In)civility vs. Political Parallelism: Studies of Content Divergence in Political Commenting Online

The recent research shows that (in)civility in online discussions has connections to both the factors that influence its use and the factors that are themselves influenced by (in)civility. The former, in their turn, may be divided into exogenous and endogenous factors.

Exogenous factors include those that influence discussions from outside. These may include platform affordances, user traits, or discussion context.

Earlier research suggests that the political stance of the media on which content users comment is also a factor that influences user discussions in various ways. These include, i.a., patterns of content spreading and sharing [59], cumulation of similar views [60], and even formation of counter-publics [61]. However, so far, the direct linkage between political parallelism of media and user incivility has not been explored. We explore whether the political stance of media affects manifestations of civility and incivility in user commenting in the Russian context.

3   Research Questions and Hypotheses

Thus, we have posed the following hypotheses:

H1. In line with previous research, the levels of incivility in both discussions will be high (over 10% of posts). The platform difference will be insignificant (less than 2%). The difference between oppositional and pro-state media will also be insignificant.
H2. The discussions have a similar configuration of incivility types, with insignificant differences between platforms and political alignments of media.
H3. Incivility is not balanced by explicit civility, which means that the volume of uncivil comments exceeds that of the civility-oriented comments at least two times on all the platforms, independent of the media's political stance.

4   Methodology and Sampling

4.1   Empirical Data

In this paper, two cases of political nature were analyzed.

The first case is the Russian pension system reform (2018). The discussions on the increase in retirement age and consequences of the Russian pension's reform were conducted most intensely during the time period from January 20, 2008 to January 24, 2019, on VK.com. Accounts in 10 Russian cities were chosen (see Table 1). According to the Ministry of Economic Development of the Russian Federation, cities are divided into the largest, large, big, medium, and small ones [63]. Thus, we selected 10 cities that would fall into these categories, represent the vast Russian territory, and have popular newsgroup accounts with live discussions. As a result, two cities with different sizes from each group were taken in order to figure out a comprehensive picture of civility and incivility in chosen social media conversations. However, the differences between cities of various sizes in terms of (in)civility were not included in analysis, as we were interested in a result that would work as a baseline. Thus, St. Petersburg and Volgograd (the largest), Kaliningrad (large), Bratsk and Nalchik (big), Belorechensk and Snezhinsk (medium), Uryupinsk and Borovichi (small) were analyzed; special attention was paid to Moscow in this study, due to the capital status of the city, but the number of comments was smaller in Moscow's discussion than in most cities' talks. A total of 5282 comments left by 431 participants were collected via parsing. We realize that such sampling is not clearly representative for any of the city groups; however, as we needed aggregated data

Table 1. The composition of the dataset on the Russian pension system reform.

City	Number of comments	Number of participants
Moscow	126	85
St. Petersburg	1793	42
Volgograd	284	67
Kaliningrad	561	38
Bratsk	120	35
Nalchik	683	27
Belorechensk	178	19
Snezhinsk	801	45
Uryupinsk	424	29
Borovichi	312	44

Table 2. Online discussions on Navalny's court verdict on the VK pages of four media outlets

Sources	Independent		Pro-state	
	Rain	Meduza	Channel One	KP.RU
Article title and contents	The suspended sentence was replaced with a real one for Navalny. Taking into account the time spent under house arrest, Navalny will spend two years and eight months in the colony.	Will Navalny's sentence be replaced with a real one? We follow what is happening in the court - and around it.	The Moscow City Court sentenced Alexei Navalny to 3.5 years in prison and a fine of 500 thousand rubles.	The court sentenced Alexei Navalny to 3.5 years in prison in a general regime colony.
Post time	02.02.2021 (20:46)	02.02.2021 (18:34)	04.02.2021 (14:03)	02.02.2021 (21:24)
N likes	499	154	116	177
N reposts	152	71	33	41
N comments	602	155	160	148

for a baseline case, the balance between feasibility and representativity allowed us to use only 10 cities of varying size for this analysis.

The target case (that of A. Navalny's court verdict in February 2021) caused a large-scale wave of opinion polarization in the Russian society. Online discussions on the pages of the VK.com social network of the politically polar Russian-language outlets were selected. These mass media outlets were chosen based on their political affiliation: openly oppositional (Rain, Meduza, by September 2022 both recognized as foreign agent entities by the Russian authorities) vs., explicitly enough, pro-state ones (Channel One, Komsomolskaya Pravda (KP.RU)). The posts with news about the court decision and user comments were all posted on February 2 to 4, 2021. In total, 1065 comments were analyzed. Table 2 presents the posts on the selected four media accounts in terms of their source and political affiliation, as well as the news piece metadata: a short textual profile of the post, its date and time, and number of likes, reposts, and comments. All the data were collected on March 10 to 15, 2021. Only the comments left strictly during February 2 to 4, 2021, were included into the dataset.

4.2 Research Methods

Despite our RQs and hypotheses being of comparative nature, this study used the case study method as it helps understand a pragmatic sense of research themes correlating with usage of (in)civility in real online discussions. Within case research, we employ the discourse analysis methodology developed by Misnikov [1] and descriptive statistics based on the results of the discourse analysis. To explore the nature of civility and incivility in the context of online conversations, we qualitatively assess patterns of their use in each case presented above. Using these methods will allow us to detect civility and incivility, which we explain in detail below.

To examine the conversations on the polarizing issues presented above, a methodological approach by Misnikov [31] was used in order to determine patterns of civil and uncivil speech in online discussions. The scientist reckons that if Internet forums can serve as public discourse structures for political expression and action, then participation in such discussions can lead to will formation and thus manifest a form of democratic citizenship for their participants. In a range of works, Misnikov suggests the standard to assess the deliberative quality of political discourse, as well as a set of empiric parameters that allow for revealing certain discursive features including civility and incivility [2–4]. His typology was used as a starting point in our analysis [1]. In this paper, the features of civil and uncivil communication were clearly distinguished and more fine-grained. As a result, the posts in both datasets were coded according to the following scheme:

1) posts mentioning a participant's name while being rude/offensive in relation to him/her, his/her nationality, religion, ideology etc. (including sarcasm);
2) posts mentioning a participant's name and rude/offensive in relation to the object of discussion;
3) posts without mentioning a participant's name but rude/offensive in relation to him/her, his/her nationality, religion, ideology, etc. (including gross sarcasm);
4) posts without mentioning a participant's name but rude/offensive in relation to the object of discussion;
5) explicitly polite and respectful posts that mention a participant's name (may contain irony, humor, or even positive sarcasm);
6) explicitly polite and respectful posts towards a person without mentioning his/her name (may contain irony, humor, or even positive sarcasm).

In order to define the level of civil and uncivil communication expressed in percentage, discussions and posts containing the features mentioned above (1–6) were analyzed and then their number of that posts was divided by the total number of posts in a discussion. To determine the general level of (in)civility in a few discussions, first, every single discussion was analyzed in terms of in(civility) described above. Second, the results with observed patterns of civil and uncivil speech in all discussions were summarized. Third, the general result was divided by the quantity of discussions.

5   Results

5.1   The Pension System Reform Case (2018)

The analysis of this case revealed a very high level of uncivil and intolerant discourse both towards the subject of discussions and their participants. The percentage of comments with uncivil speech (34.33%, towards both the participants and the subject discussed) was nearly 1.5 times higher than that of openly civil, polite, and respectful comments (23.44%) (see Table 3).

Table 3. Presence of civility and incivility in the public VK pages on the pensions reform

Types of speech		Comments, %
Civil speech	Explicitly polite and respectful posts towards participants addressed by name or personal expressions (they can include irony, humor, sarcasm of non-offensive character)	8.31
	Posts do not include an explicit mention of participants' name, they are explicitly polite and respectful (including intentional politeness, irony, humor or sarcasm of non-offensive character)	15.13
Uncivil speech	Obviously rude or offensive posts towards person, nationality, religion, ideology, place of living addressed by name or personal expressions (differ from irony/humor/sarcasm)	9.29
	Posts do not include an explicit mention of participants' name, they contain obviously rude or abusive expressions and vocabulary (irony, humor and sarcasm are excluded)	7.69
	Posts are dedicated directly or indirectly to the pension reform, they are on subject but rude towards a certain person	4.03
	Posts are dedicated directly or indirectly to pension reform, they are on subject but rude, impersonal	13.32

5.2   The Navalny's Court Sentence Case (2021)

Table 4 shows that openly tolerant and intentionally civil speech was virtually absent from user comments under both pro-state and oppositional/independent media, cross-validating our previous results on incivility as playing a bigger role in constituting the fabric of polar online discussions [23]. The impolite, rude attitude towards the participants, as well as towards the subject of discussion, strongly prevailed over polite ones as shown by the percentage of the posts with rude attitude towards other participants in all the discussions.

Table 4. Analysis of civility and incivility in the VK discussions on Navalny's court verdict

Types of speech		Independent		Pro-state		Mean
		Rain	Meduza	Channel One	KP.RU	
Civil speech	Posts with participant name's mention, discussion on topic in a polite in a tolerant way	0	0	0	0	0.7
	Posts without participant name's mention, discussion on topic in a tolerant way	0	0	0	0	0
Uncivil speech	Posts with participant name' mention, discussion on topic, but rude towards participants	**9.1**	4.5	2.5	2	4.53
	Posts with participant name's mention, discussion on topic but rude towards the subject of discussion	0.7	0.7	**3.1**	2	1.63
	Posts without a participant name's mention, discussion on topic but rude towards participants	0.3	**1.9**	1.3	0.7	1.1
	Posts without a participant name's mention, discussion on topic, but rude towards the subject of discussion	1.8	1.9	1.3	**4.7**	2.43
	Total % of incivility towards participants	**9.4**	6.4	3.8	2.7	5.58
	Total % of incivility towards the object of discussion	2.5	2.6	4.4	**6.7**	4.1
	Total % of civil and uncivil speech	11.9	9	8.2	9.4	9.6

However, the overall percentages of uncivil comments were also much lower than in the case of the pension reform. The total sum of uncivil comments in the discussions on non-mediatized VK.com is 2.8 to 4.2 times higher than under the posts of the legacy media. Thus, we see that media presence and their initiation of discussions play a crucial role in diminishing both the open civility and open incivility of online speech.

We have also shown that commenters of independent media are more correlated with counterpart discussants, while the users who commented on pro-state media preferred to attack the object of discussion. This suggests us that the pattern of less controlled speech being more inclined to criticizing the discussion participants – this both raises the quality of discussions (via hinting on higher dialogicity) and lowers it, as attacks towards fellow participants do not lead to meaningful discussion. The higher number of comments that criticize the object of discussion (the problem itself) was higher on pro-state media, which reflects on simultaneously of lesser freedom of discussion in terms of addressing, even if aggressively, fellow commenters, and of higher discussion quality more oriented to issue-based discourse. This needs to be researched further, as this result partly reshapes our understanding of how uncivil speech works regard to media bias.

At the same time, the overall difference between the volume of uncivil speech in pro-state and independent media was too small to make conclusions about their stable difference. The highest percentage of uncivil comments was detected for the Rain TV's viewers and commenters (11.9%), while the lowest number of 8.2% was found for Channel One, the difference in the number of comments being only 3.7%. Thus, we can make an important conclusion that, on social networks, political parallelism does shape incivility of discussions; however, not in terms of the volume of uncivil commenting but in terms of the addressees of incivility, which definitely calls for future studies.

5.3 Responding to the Hypotheses

In terms of our hypotheses, we can state the following.

H1 (on the volume of uncivil speech) is strongly supported for the VK.com public pages but not for media where the results fluctuate around 10% (from 8.2% to 11.9%). With regard to platform difference (public pages or media accounts), H1 is strongly rejected, as the result for the former is 2.8 to 4.2 times higher than for the latter. For the difference between media of various bias, formally, H1 is supported, as the biggest difference has reached 3.7% (higher than the 2% threshold). However, we still consider this difference not that substantial, especially in comparison with the results for public pages on VK.com.

H2 on the patterns of distribution of types of uncivil speech is, in general, not supported, as the pattern for the pensions reform repeats for neither of the four media. This indicates that independent dynamics of incivility on 'open' VK.com and on media spaces within VK.com, and of absence of any generalizable patterns for all media represented on the platform.

H3, though, is supported, as incivility is not balanced via open civility. And if, on the public pages, incivility is not balanced *enough*, on the media pages, it is not balanced *at all*. This deserves expanding our research to look for the reasons of generally more neutral user speech on media pages present on VK.com.

6   Discussion and Conclusion

In this paper, we have investigated the balance between civil and uncivil speech on Russian social media discussions (represented by VK.com) on the pension system reform and on the court verdict for Alexey Navalny in relation to political parallelism of media outlets present on social networks.

Our study had several limitations. First, more data is needed to perform descriptive statistics and measure the validity of our claims via statistical means; in this paper, we can only claim trends that we see in the data, not statistically proven dependencies. However, even such results deserve scholarly attention, as political parallelism of media has not previously been in the focus of the academe, to our best knowledge, while it shapes the structure of consensus online. Second, more analysis should be provided on interactivity of users, as there can be hyperactive and dominant participants who shape discussions and have an impact on them in terms of civil and uncivil patterns. This aspect should be taken into account in the future research in order to obtain more objective outcomes. Third, our method of manual coding needs to be complemented or substituted where possible by machine-learning techniques and automated detection of (in)civility. Fourth, the method by Misnikov may need to be expanded and/or corrected, in order to account for non-deliberative nature of user utterances.

We obtained some results according to our hypotheses that, on the one hand, are based on the previous research works, and, on other one, are aimed at developing new ideas and directions of research thought in the future studies. Thus, the analysis demonstrated high levels of incivility in political communication online as over 10% of posts on VK.com platforms contained intolerant, offensive and rude expressions both towards participants and subject of deliberating (**H1**). Referring to platform difference, the outcomes of target case's analysis showed insignificant distinction between them (**H1**). In addition, there was not much diversity in incivility between oppositional and pro-state media, but it was higher than 2% in most cases (**H1**). These conclusions are cross-validated by the outcomes of previous research conducted on Russian [23] and Belarusian YouTube [25] where an important role of incivility as a marker of strong opinion polarization in mass-scale online political discussions was formulated.

The discussions have dissimilar configurations of incivility types in absolute figures, but the low number of uncivil comments on legacy media accounts makes differences between platforms and political alignments of media insignificant (**H2**). This observation may contribute to the future studies dedicated to freedom of opinion expression in civil or uncivil manner and the hate speech dilemma which are partly developed in some previous works (see [12, 14, 23, 58, 59]).

Incivility is not balanced by explicit civility, which means that the volume of uncivil comments exceeds that of the civility-oriented comments at least two times on all the platforms, independent of the media's political stance (**H3**). For example, the analysis of (in)civility using the case of pension reform system case showed 34.33% of uncivil patterns vs. 23.44% of civil ones, the Navalny's court sentence case – a more unbalanced proportion – 9.69% vs. 0.18% respectively. Considering the media's political stance in the target case, we observed hint to the 'free speech vs. hate speech' dilemma, as the comments in the oppositional media appear to be more hostile but also more diverse in opinion expression, while those on the pro-state accounts look less polluted by aggression and offense but show signs of stronger filter bubbles (**H3**). However, the difference in the level of incivility between discussions on the VK pages of oppositional and pro-state media outlets was irrelevant (**H3**). This finding may merit future research on political parallelism expressed via (un)civil speech and political parallelism's effects in traditional and social media.

To put our results in further context, we may say that we had done some research on American culture of communication in terms of (in)civility [14]. For example, we looked at the case of the second impeachment of Donald Trump and how citizens discussed it on Facebook groups of politically polar media. As a result, in general, there were more civil and polite expressions towards both the participants and the discussed topic. For the US dataset, we came to the conclusion that the political stance of media played a role in opinion formation, as well as in the arguments and manner opinions cumulate. There, we detected 'direct' parallelism when participants of discussions on Facebook pages of liberal media outlets spoke more negatively on the object of discussion (Donald Trump) than on the conservative media. Interestingly, for the USA, our conclusion on larger-scale presence of incivility in more pro-democratic and free media is also true, with the culture of communication being more intolerant on liberal media's accounts than those of the participants of conservative media. The discussions on platforms of liberal media outlets were more reasoned than on platforms of conservative ones, but less interactive and dialogical. This clearly sets a comparative perspective for the studies like ours, as we have seen a different nature of polarization between oppositional and pro-state media in Russia,

Thus, in further research, both the forms of incivility and their relation to the outer context (e.g., represented by the offline media system) should be investigated in more detail. Moreover, it is relevant to consider a correlation between uncivil traits of users' behavior and their disagreement patterns, since it may provide a better understanding whether incivility provokes disagreement and in what fashion it has an impact on it. One more research field is that different platforms for e-deliberation may demonstrate different levels and forms of uncivil patterns due to the specific affordances of digital environments, possibilities they open for communicating, and their biases.

Acknowledgements. The research was supported by the Russian Science Foundation grant No. 22-18-00364 «Institutional Transformation of E-Participation Governance in Russia: a Study of Regional Peculiarities» (https://rscf.ru/project/22-18-00364/) and grant No. 21-18-00454 «Mediatized Communication and Modern Deliberative Process» (https://www.rscf.ru/project/21-18-00454/). The case of verdict court to A. Navalny was done in terms of grant No. 22-18-00364, the case of pension reform – grant No. 21-18-00454.

References

1. Pfetsch, B.: Dissonant and disconnected public spheres as challenge for political communication research. Javnost – The Public **25**, 1–2, 59–65 (2018)
2. Bodrunova, S.: Social media and political dissent in Russia and Belarus: an introduction to the special issue. Social Media + Society **7**(4), 20563051211063470 (2021)
3. Bodrunova, S.S.: Practices of cumulative deliberation: a meta-review of the recent research findings. In: Chugunov, A.V., Janssen, M., Khodachek, I., Misnikov, Y., Trutnev, D. (eds.) EGOSE 2021. CCIS, vol. 1529, pp. 89–104. Springer, Cham (2022). https://doi.org/10.1007/978-3-031-04238-6_8

4. Bodrunova, S.S., Blekanov, I.S., Maksimov, A.: Public opinion dynamics in online discussions: cumulative commenting and micro-level spirals of silence. In: Meiselwitz, G. (ed.) HCII 2021. LNCS, vol. 12774, pp. 205–220. Springer, Cham (2021). https://doi.org/10.1007/978-3-030-77626-8_14
5. Moy, P., Gastil, J.: Predicting deliberative conversation: the impact of discussion networks, media use, and political cognitions. Polit. Commun. **23**(4), 443–460 (2006)
6. Stromer-Galley, J.: Measuring deliberation's content: a coding scheme. J. Public Deliberation **3**, 1–35 (2007)
7. Jamieson, K., Hardy, B.: What is civil engaged argument and why does aspiring to it matter? In: Shea, D.M., Fiorina, M. (eds.) Can We Talk? The Rise of Rude, Nasty, Stubborn Politics, pp. 27– 40. Pearson Press, Upper Saddle River (2012)
8. Boatright, R., Shaffer, T., Sobieraj, S., Young, D. (eds.): A Crisis of Civility?: Political Discourse and Its Discontents, 1st edn. Routledge (2019)
9. Kurtz, H.: Hannity-Ellison dustup shows our broken politics, CNN (2013). http://www.cnn.com/2013/03/01/opinion/kurtz-hannity-ellison-dust-up
10. Boyd, R.: The value of civility? Urban Stud. **43**, 863–878 (2006). https://doi.org/10.1080/00420980600676105
11. Papacharissi, Z.: Democracy online: civility, politeness, and the democratic potential of online political discussion groups. New Media Soc. **6**(2), 259–283 (2004)
12. Volkovskii, D.: Experience of applied research in online deliberation: an analysis of civility in American online discussions. In: International Conference "Internet and Modern Society", IMS 2021, St. Petersburg, Russia, 24–26 June 2021, pp. 199–205 (2021)
13. Filatova, O., Volkovskii, D.: Online deliberation on social media as a form of public dialogue in Russia. In: International Conference "Internet and Modern Society", IMS 2021, St. Petersburg, Russia, 24–26 June 2021, pp. 146–156 (2021)
14. Volkovskii, D., Filatova, O.: Influence of media type on political E-discourse: analysis of Russian and American discussions on social media. In: Chugunov, A.V., Janssen, M., Khodachek, I., Misnikov, Y., Trutnev, D. (eds.) EGOSE 2021. CCIS, vol. 1529, pp. 119–131. Springer, Cham (2022). https://doi.org/10.1007/978-3-031-04238-6_10
15. Herbst, S.: Rude Democracy: Civility and Incivility in American Politics. Temple University Press, Philadelphia (2010)
16. Rowe, I.: Civility 2.0: a comparative analysis of incivility in online political discussion. Inf. Commun. Soc. **18**, 121–138 (2015)
17. Sobieraj, S., Berry, J.: From incivility to outrage: political discourse in blogs, talk radio, and cable news. Polit. Commun. **28**, 19–41 (2011)
18. Coe, K., Kenski, K., Rains, S.: Online and uncivil? Patterns and determinants of incivility in newspaper website comments. J. Commun. **64**, 659–679 (2014)
19. Pluzer-Sarno, A.: Materny slovar' kak fenomen russkoy kultury [Mat vocabulary as a phenomenon of Russian culture]. Novaya russkaya kniga, Moscow (2000)
20. Malyuga, E.N., Orlova, S.N.: Theoretical concepts and notions of Euphemy. In: Malyuga, E.N., Orlova, S.N. (eds.) Linguistic Pragmatics of Intercultural Professional and Business Communication, pp. 79–103. Springer, Cham (2018). https://doi.org/10.1007/978-3-319-68744-5_3
21. Salimovsky, V.A., Ermakova, L.M.: Ekstremistskiy diskurs v massovoy kommunikatsii Runeta[Extremist discourse in Runet mass communication]. Rossiyskaya i zarubezhnaya filologia **3**(15), 71–80 (2011)
22. Vendil Pallin, C.: Internet control through ownership: the case of Russia. Post-Soviet Affairs **33**(1), 16–33 (2017)
23. Bodrunova, S.S., Litvinenko, A., Blekanov, I., Nepiyushchikh, D.: Constructive aggression? Multiple roles of aggressive content in political discourse on Russian YouTube. Media Commun. **9**, 181–194 (2021)

24. Massaro, T.M.: Equality and freedom of expression: the hate speech dilemma. William & Mary Law Rev. **32** (1990). https://scholarship.law.wm.edu/cgi/viewcontent.cgi?referer=https://www.google.com/&httpsredir=1&article=1923&context=wmlr
25. Bodrunova, S., Blekanov, I.: A self-critical public: cumulation of opinion on Belarusian oppositional YouTube before the 2020 protests. Soc. Media + Soc. **7**(1), 1–13 (2021)
26. Mancini, P.: Instrumentalization of the media vs. political parallelism. Chin. J. Commun. **5**(3), 262–280 (2012)
27. De Albuquerque, A.: Political parallelism. In: Oxford Research Encyclopedia of Communication (2018)
28. Bodrunova, S., Litvinenko, A.: Fragmentation of society and media hybridisation in today's Russia: how Facebook voices collective demands. Zhurnal Issledovanii Sotsial'noi Politiki (J. Soc. Policy Res.) **14**(1), 113–124 (2016)
29. Bodrunova, S.S., Litvinenko, A.A., Blekanov, I.S.: Influencers on the Russian Twitter: institutions vs. people in the discussion on migrants. In: Proceedings of the International Conference on Electronic Governance and Open Society: Challenges in Eurasia, pp. 212–222 (2016)
30. Litvinenko, A.: YouTube as alternative television in Russia: political videos during the presidential election campaign 2018. Soc. Media + Soc. **7**(1), 2056305120984455 (2021)
31. Misnikov, Y.: Public Activism Online in Russia: Citizens' Participation in Web-based Interactive Political Debate in the Context of Civil Society. Development and Transition to Democracy: Ph.D. thesis … Ph. D./Leeds (2011)
32. Filatova, O., Kabanov, Y., Misnikov, Y.: Public deliberation in Russia: deliberative quality, rationality and interactivity of the online media discussions. Media Commun. **7**(3), 133–144 (2019)
33. Bodrunova, S.S.: The boundaries of context: contextual knowledge in research on networked discussions. In: Antonyuk, A., Basov, N. (eds.) NetGloW 2020. LNNS, vol. 181, pp. 165–179. Springer, Cham (2021). https://doi.org/10.1007/978-3-030-64877-0_11
34. Habermas, J.: Between Facts and Norms. Contributions to a Discourse Theory of Law and Democracy. MIT Press, Cambridge (1996)
35. Dahlberg, L.: The Internet and democratic discourse: exploring the prospects of online deliberative forums for extending the public sphere. Inf. Commun. Soc. **4**(4), 615–633 (2001)
36. Delli Carpini, M., Cook, F., Jacobs, L.: Public deliberation, discursive participation, and civic engagement: a review of the empirical literature. Annu. Rev. Polit. Sci. **7**, 315–344 (2004)
37. Gastil, J., Deess, E., Weiser, P.: Civic awakening in the jury room: a test of the connection between jury deliberation and political participation. J. Polit. **64**, 585–595 (2002)
38. Min, S.-J.: Online vs. face-to-face deliberation: effects on civic engagement. J. Comput.-Mediated Commun. **12**, 1369–1387 (2007)
39. Laden, A.: Two Concepts of Civility. A Crisis of Civility? Routledge, New York (2019)
40. Stuckey, M., O'Rourke, S.: Civility, democracy, and national politics. Rhetoric Public Aff. **17**(4), Winter 2014, 711–736 (2014)
41. Zurn, C.: Political civility: another illusionistic ideal. Public Aff. Q. **27**(4), 341–368 (2013)
42. Reiheld, A.: Asking too much? Civility vs. pluralism. Philos. Top. **41**(2), 59–78 (2013)
43. Rood, C.: Rhetorics of civility: theory, pedagogy, and practice in speaking and writing textbooks. Rhetor. Rev. **32**(3), 331–348 (2014)
44. Mutz, D.: Hearing the Other Side: Deliberative Versus Participatory Democracy. Cambridge University Press, New York (2006)
45. Mutz, D., Reeves, B.: The new videomalaise: effects of televised incivility on political trust. Am. Polit. Sci. Rev. **99**, 1–15 (2005)
46. Ng, E., Detenber, B.: The impact of synchronicity and civility in online political discussions on perceptions and intentions to participate. J. Comput.-Mediated Commun. **10**(3) (2005)
47. Benson, T.: The rhetoric of civility: power, authenticity, and democracy. J. Contemp. Rhetoric **1**(1), 22–30 (2011)

48. Stryker, R., Conway, B., Danielson, J.: What is political incivility? Commun. Monogr. **83**, 535–556 (2016)
49. Vollhardt, J., Coutin, M., Staub, E., Weiss, G., Deflander, J.: Deconstructing hate speech in the DRC: a psycho-logical media sensitization campaign. J. Hate Stud. **5**, 15–36 (2007)
50. Miller, M., Vaccari, C.: Digital threats to democracy: comparative lessons and possible remedies. Int. J. Press/Polit. **25**(3), 333–356 (2020)
51. Anderson, A., Brossard, D., Scheufele, D., Xenos, M., Ladwig, P.: The "nasty effect:" online incivility and risk perceptions of emerging technologies. J. Comput.-Mediat. Commun. **19**(3), 373–387 (2014)
52. Hmielowski, J., Hutchens, M., Cicchirillo, V.: Living in an age of online incivility: examining the conditional indirect effects of online discussion on political flaming. Inf. Commun. Soc. (2014)
53. Hwang, H., Kim, Y., Huh, C.: Seeing is believing: effects of uncivil online debate on political polarization and expectations of deliberation. J. Broadcast. Electron. Media **58**, 621–633 (2014)
54. Kim, Y., Kim, Y.: Incivility on Facebook and political polarization: the mediating role of seeking further comments and negative emotion. Comput. Hum. Behav. **99**, 219–227 (2019)
55. Gervais, B.: Following the news? Reception of uncivil partisan media and the use of incivility in political expression. Polit. Commun. **31**, 564–583 (2014)
56. Han, S.-H., Brazeal, L.: Playing nice: modeling civility in online political discussions. Commun. Res. Rep. **32**, 20–28 (2015)
57. McClurg, S.: Political disagreement in context: the conditional effect of neighborhood context, disagreement and political talk on electoral participation. Polit. Behav. **28**, 349–366 (2006)
58. Nigmatullina, K., Rodossky, N.: Social media engagement anxiety: triggers in news agenda. In: Meiselwitz, G. (ed.) Social Computing and Social Media: Design, User Experience and Impact: SCSM 2022, pp. 345–357. Springer, Cham (2022). https://doi.org/10.1007/978-3-031-05061-9_25
59. Casteltrione, I., Pieczka, M.: Mediating the contributions of Facebook to political participation in Italy and the UK: the role of media and political landscapes. Palgrave Commun. **4**(1), 1–11 (2018)
60. Gilbert, E., Bergstrom, T., Karahalios, K.: Blogs are echo chambers: blogs are echo chambers. In: 2009 42nd Hawaii International Conference on System Sciences, pp. 1–10. IEEE (2009)
61. Toepfl, F., Piwoni, E.: Public spheres in interaction: comment sections of news websites as counterpublic spaces. J. Commun. **65**(3), 465–488 (2015)
62. Savin, N.: Does media matter? Variation of VK and Facebook deliberative capacities (evidence from discussions on the Crimea crisis). Commun. Media Des. **4**(3), 119–139 (2019)
63. Ministerstvo ekonomicheskogo razvitia Rossiyskoi Federazii. SP 42.13330.2011 Gradostoi-telstvo. Planirovka i zastroika gorodskih i selskih poselenii. Aktualizirovannaya redaczia SNiP 2.07.01–89. [Ministry of Economic Development of the Russian Federation. SR 42.13330.2011 Urban development. Planning and building of urban and rural settlements. Updated edition 2.07.01–89] (2011)

Data and Network Security

Federated Learning for the Efficient Detection of Steganographic Threats Hidden in Image Icons

Nunziato Cassavia[1] , Luca Caviglione[2] , Massimo Guarascio[1]([✉]) ,
Angelica Liguori[3] , Giuseppe Surace[3], and Marco Zuppelli[2]

[1] Institute for High Performance Computing and Networking, Rende, Italy
{nunziato.cassavia,massimo.guarascio}@icar.cnr.it
[2] Institute for Applied Mathematics and Information Technologies, Genova, Italy
{luca.caviglione,marco.zuppelli}@ge.imati.cnr.it
[3] University of Calabria, Rende, Italy
angelica.liguori@dimes.unical.it

Abstract. An increasing number of threat actors takes advantage of
information hiding techniques to prevent detection or to drop payloads
containing attack routines. With the ubiquitous diffusion of mobile applications, high-resolution icons should be considered a very attractive car-
rier for cloaking malicious information via steganographic mechanisms.
Despite machine learning approaches proven to be effective to detect
hidden payloads, the mobile scenario could challenge their deployment
in realistic use cases, for instance due to scalability constraints. Therefore, this paper introduces an approach based on federated learning able
to prevent hazards characterizing production-quality scenarios, including
different privacy regulations and lack of comprehensive datasets. Numerical results indicate that our approach achieves performances similar to
those of centralized solutions.

Keywords: Federated Learning · Information Hiding · Deep
Learning · Malware Detection

1 Introduction

Among the various techniques used by threat actors to distribute malicious payloads and update configuration of malware, the adoption of steganography is
becoming a consolidated practice [2]. Despite the hiding process may vary, e.g.,
it can target network traffic to bypass intrusion detection systems or shared
hardware resources to allow processes to elude sandboxes, digital images are the
most effective and adopted carriers [14]. For instance, a recent attack campaign
exploited steganography to drop a malicious Golang executable on the host of
the victim. To this aim, the malware has been cloaked in security certificates of

C. Comito and D. Talia (Eds.): PerSOM 2022, LNICST 494, pp. 83–95, 2023.
https://doi.org/10.1007/978-3-031-31469-8_6

pictures taken by the James Webb space telescope. As a consequence of effective advancements in offensive approaches, a surge in the volume of attacks has been observed and threat actors can now endanger almost any device or host, for instance to distribute ransomware [18]. To face such a challenging scenario, security should be enforced from the very early phases of the development process (e.g., by means of by-design approaches) as well as in the various stages of the distribution pipeline.

Unfortunately, typical countermeasures could not be sufficient to mitigate threats exploiting information hiding techniques, especially when targeting mobile devices [3]. Prime evidences on the effectiveness of image steganography to elude standard security checks can be rooted back to 2014. In this case, attackers concealed secret data by exploiting digital media contained in applications made available through the Google Play Store [23]. Indeed, machine learning frameworks are becoming key tools to partially mitigate the impact of threats exploiting advanced offensive schemes [4]. For instance, they demonstrated to be effective for checking the behaviors of mobile applications, which are usually based on a complex interplay of software components [28].

Therefore, along the lines of [1], this paper addresses the problem of revealing malicious payloads hidden within high-resolution icons that are commonly used in most popular mobile ecosystems, including, Android and iOS. Despite machine learning approaches proven to be effective to spot several offensive techniques based on obfuscation and information hiding (see, e.g., [4] and [6]), deploying such frameworks in real-world scenarios could be unfeasible. For instance, resource-intensive computations may not be possible in a centralized manner, due to scalability constraints, lack of suitable datasets, or the use of a multitude of shared libraries and software components [16, 29]. As a workaround, this paper introduces a supervised approach exploiting federated learning. As observed in many settings, computation can be distributed across multiple cloud replicas or edge nodes, which can cooperate to the definition of models by exploiting local information (e.g., crawled from the Internet or gathered from "unofficial" application stores). Moreover, the federated approach could prevent GDPR-like hazards due to processing operations performed in areas with conflicting policies about data confidentiality [19].

Summing up, the contribution of this paper is the design and the performance evaluation of a federated approach that allows multiple "app stores" to cooperate for revealing the presence of applications bundled with steganographic threats.

The rest of the paper is structured as follows. Section 2 reviews past works considering federated approaches for counteracting malware, whereas Sect. 3 introduces the reference scenario. Section 4 deals with the framework, while Sect. 5 showcases numerical results obtained through simulations. Finally, Sect. 6 concludes the paper and portraits some possible future research directions.

2   Related Works

Enforcing security of mobile applications usually relies upon a variety of techniques (e.g., static binary analysis, anomaly-based detection, enforcement of policies in end nodes), which require a strict cooperation among developers, users and administrators of application stores [7]. In general, the current trend takes advantage of some form of machine learning or artificial intelligence to analyze behaviors of software, exploit existent attack signatures and reveal unexpected interactions among applications or their components[1]. For the specific case of attacks leveraging information hiding to target digital media, machine learning confirmed its effectiveness, especially to support the steganalysis process that can drive the neutralization of cloaked data [15]. Unfortunately, the application of machine-learning-capable techniques often clashes with some practical constraints. First, the inspection of bundled assets and copyrighted material should be designed in order to respect privacy-enforcing regulations, or by relying on architectures that do not process any personal information [20]. Second, the mobile ecosystem is growing on a continuous basis, thus leading to millions of samples to verify. An application can be made available also via different store replica for performance purposes or through unofficial channels (e.g., alternative stores or via sideloading). As a result, the creation of comprehensive datasets is a hard task [25]. To partially cope with such drawbacks, federated approaches are becoming a prime tool, see, e.g., [21] for a thorough discussion even if focused on the case of IoT ecosystems.

For the specific case of revealing contents cloaked in digital images via distributed frameworks, [27] exploits federated transfer learning to improve the performance of image steganalysis while preserving the privacy of users. Even if the work partially overlaps with our idea, the considered scenario is completely different, i.e., it considers end nodes instead of applications stores and does not focus on real attacks or malware samples. For the case of using federated learning to tame realistic threats, the literature offers various attempts. As an example, [12] showcases a framework for enabling end nodes running Android to classify several types of malware, including ransomware and spyware but not steganographic threats. The problem of classifying malicious samples is also addressed in [13], which considers a generic scenario not related to security of mobile applications. Instead, [22] addresses the problem of detecting malware but limited to an OS no longer used (i.e., Symbian S60) and does not consider application stores or modern software distribution pipelines.

A possible "meet in the middle" blueprint offloads end nodes towards edge entities placed at the border of the network. In this case, cooperating stores could resembles such an architecture. However, the literature does not offer prior attempts based on edge computing to reveal the presence of threats endowed with information hiding or image steganography capabilities. In fact, this paradigm, jointly with federated techniques, has been largely used in IoT scenarios often composed of resource-constrained nodes [24]. Besides, for the specific case of mobile security, edge/federated approaches have been mainly adopted to guarantee privacy constraints. As a paradigmatic example, [11] demonstrates how to detect malware without exposing sensitive information of end users, such as configuration details or how various application program interfaces are invoked.

---

[1] Cloud-based protection mechanisms at the basis of the Google Play Protect framework: https://developers.google.com/android/play-protect/cloud-based-protections.

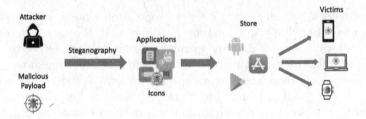

Fig. 1. Reference attack scenario considered in this work.

3   Attack Model and Federated Approach

The general attack model considered in this work deals with a threat actor wanting to hide a malicious payload within icons of applications by using steganography. Such a scheme could be exploited to make the reverse engineering of the attack chain harder or to distribute additional assets (e.g., configurations, URLs or small scripts) without triggering standard security mechanisms, such as those based on signatures or the static analysis of software. Each icon is then "repacked" within an application and then published through a store to make it available to users. Figure 1 depicts the reference attack scenario. To hide the malicious payload, we consider an attacker using the plain Least Significant Bit (LSB) technique, which has been observed in various real-world campaigns [2,14]. In essence, LSB allows to alter the least significant bit(s) of the color components of each pixel of the container image to conceal a secret. We point out that, the more bits are altered, the higher the chance of revealing the presence of the hidden payload via visible alterations or artifacts. To mitigate such an attack, there is the need of deploying a suitable scheme within the store to "reveal" the presence of hidden data and prevent that a malicious application is delivered. See [1] for a detailed discussion of a possible architecture using a centralized blueprint.

To detect the hidden data, we leverage a federated-learning-based approach to learn a global, optimal model in a distributed fashion. Figure 2 depicts our reference architecture. In the following, to prevent the need of formal definitions, we will refer to the centralized store as the server. Similarly, with end nodes we will identify other (groups of) machines located in the Internet and cooperating towards the distribution of applications and the detection process. In more detail, we assume that the server contains various mobile applications along with their icons, e.g., it can be considered an "app store". To prevent computational or security hazards, the server also contains pointers to some applications acting as a sort of "cache", for instance for the most popular contents. Instead, the end nodes represent local datacenters containing a subset of applications/icons already present in the main store and replicated for redundancy. Moreover, end nodes can also contain novel/unseen data, e.g., collected from third-part markets. To spot the presence of an application/icon hiding a malicious content, end nodes and the server collaborate to find the optimal DNN-based model via a federated

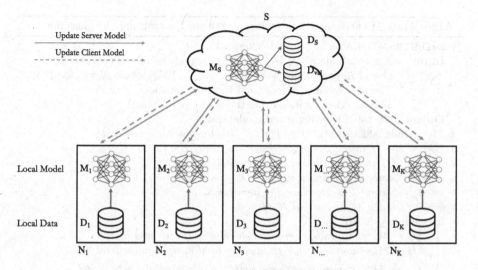

Fig. 2. Federated approach of cooperating stores.

approach. As discussed, such strategies are mainly used to avoid moving raw data from end nodes to the server, to take advantage of the computational capabilities of each node, and to guarantee the privacy of local devices.

Referring again to Fig. 2, we suppose to have a centralized server denoted as S in the figure. The server contains a "weak" DNN detector model M_S trained on an initial dataset D_S and validated through the validation set D_{val}. At the beginning, the detector is shared across K end nodes, which then fine-tune their model M_i against the local data D_i. To make the predictor more robust and to find a global model in a distributed manner, a subset of end nodes periodically sends updates to the server S containing the weights of each layer composing their local DNN. The server S aggregates the information received to obtain an ensemble model, which is validated against the validation set. If the model performs better with respect to the previous one, then the server sends back the best parameters to the end nodes. This process is iterated until a certain convergence criteria is reached. More formally, Algorithm 1 details the federated learning algorithm for training the malware classifier. As regards the procedures to yield the ensemble model `CreateSoupModel` and to fine-tune both global and local models `FineTune`, they are fully described in Sect. 4.3.

4   Framework

In this section, we first illustrate the methodology used to detect and classify compromised images, then we describe the neural architecture devised to tackle these problems. Finally we present the ensemble solution adopted in our FL-based approach to combine the different neural models yielded by end nodes.

Algorithm 1: (Federated) Learning algorithm for training the classifier.

---

1 BuildFLModel(S,N,*max_iter*,*eval_criterion*)

   Input : A server node $S = \{M_S, D_S, D_{val}\}$ acting the role of coordinator

          List of K peer nodes $N = [N_1, \ldots, N_i, \ldots, N_K]$ where $N_i = \{M_i, D_i\}$

          The max number of federated learning iterations *max_iter*

          The criterion for measuring the model performances *eval_criterion*

   Output: federated learning based model BM

2 M_S = InduceNNModel(D_S) // *build a detector against server data*

3 $BM = M_S$ // *initialize the best federated model BM*

4 $M_N = [\,]$ // *initialize the list of peer models*

5 Q_{BM} = ComputePerformances(BM, D_{val}, *eval_criterion*)

6 $i = 0$ // *current federated learning iteration*

7 $k = 0$ // *index of the current Node*

8 **foreach** $k \leq K$ **do**

9      $M_k = M_S$ // *download server model and initialize local model*

10   M_k = FineTune(M_k, D_k) // *finetune local model against local data*

11     $M_N \overset{+}{\leftarrow} M_k$ // *share local model with S and append the k-th model*

12     $k = k + 1$

13 **end**

14 M_S = CreateSoupModel(M_N, D_S) // *create an ensemble model*

15 Q_{M_S} = ComputePerformances(M_S, D_{val}, *eval_criterion*)

16 **if** $Q_{BM} \leq Q_{M_S}$ **then**

17     $BM = M_S$

18     $Q_{BM} = Q_{M_S}$

19 **end**

20 **if** $i \leq max\_iter$ **then**

21     $M_S = [\,]$ // *clean the list of peer models*

22     $i = i + 1$

23   **go to** line 7

24 **end**

25 **return** BM

4.1 Solution Approach

Figure 3 depicts the general methodology leveraged to cope with the problem of discovering images targeted via steganographic methods. Specifically, digital images represent the input of the proposed approach and are modeled as matrices with dimension $X \times Y$. The pixel is the smallest manageable element of these matrices and stores information about the color. The color of each pixel can be decomposed into three main components i.e., Red (R), Green (G) and Blue (B). As hinted, in this work we focus on high-resolution icons as they offer a sort of "unified playground" for various threats. At the same time, this does not account for a loss of generality, as the approach can be applied and scaled also to address regular-sized images. In the following, we then consider that the values associated to RGB components represent the intensity of the various colors and

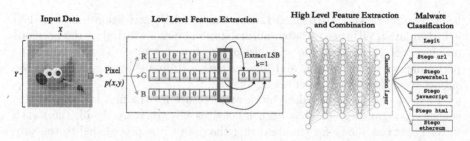

Fig. 3. Methodological approach for the classification of a stegomalware cloaked in a digital image via LSB steganography.

each value ranges in the interval $[0, 255]$. Hereinafter, we denote with N the size of the image computed as $N = X \times Y \times 3$.

Concerning the hiding method, LSB steganography represents a prominent approach to hide malicious code or data in legitimate pictures by changing the value of the (k) least significant bit(s) of each color composing the pixel of the image (see, Fig. 3 for the case of $k = 1$). When only a limited number of changes are performed on the image, it will not exhibit any visible alteration, i.e., pixels will look homogeneous compared to the surrounding elements [30]. As a consequence, many approaches proposed in the literature partially fail to detect the presence of hidden content as they produce weak detection models unable to discover the slight differences between licit and compromised contents.

To address all these issues, in this work we devised a (Federated) Deep Learning approach that processes and analyzes the k LSBs of the image icons under investigation. Basically, the first block of the proposed neural network is devoted to yield a flat representation of the image by extracting the k least significant bits of each pixel. Such a representation is then propagated to the subsequent layers to detect/classify different malicious contents. The DNN allows to extract high-level discriminative features to be further combined for producing the final classification.

4.2 Neural Architecture

To mitigate the impact of threats leveraging information hiding, we designed a supervised neural architecture for the classification task of image icons. In more detail, we exploited the deep architectures shown in Fig. 4, which permits to produce reliable predictions. Essentially, our neural architecture is composed of a stack of several blocks. The first layer acts as an handler for the input provided to the network (denoted as `Input Handler` in Fig. 4) and propagates the information (i.e., the image) to the subsequent layers of the DNN for further processing. The second component (denoted as `Low Level Feature Extraction` in Fig. 4) yields a flat representation of the image and extracts the raw information by means of a masking procedure.

The overall DNN is composed of a variable number m of `Building Block BB` obtained by stacking three main components: *(i)* on top, a fully-connected dense layer (equipped with a Rectified Linear Unit (ReLU) activation function [17]) is instantiated, *(ii)* then, a batch-normalization layer is stacked to the previous one in order to improve the stability of the learning phase and to boost the performances of the model, and finally, *(iii)* a dropout layer is added to the subnet to mitigate the risk of overfitting [9].

Figure 4 details the building block architecture for the first instance of this specific configuration and has been labeled as `BB₁`. In more detail, the `Batch Normalization` allows for standardizing the data to be propagated to the subsequent layers of the DNN with respect to the current batch (by considering the average μ and the variance σ of each input). A reset of a random number of neurons in the training phase is performed via a dropout mechanism. As pinpointed in [10], the usage of the dropout method induces in the DNN a behavior similar to an ensemble model. Hence, the overall output of the whole neural network can be considered as the combination of different sub-networks resulting from this random masking, which disables some paths of the neural architecture.

In our experiments the neural model is instantiated with $m = 4$ building blocks. The proposed neural classifier also includes a skip connection to implement a residual block. The usage of the skip connections induces in the base DNN classifier a behavior similar to *Residual Networks* [8], which demonstrated to be effective solutions to the well-known *degradation problem* (i.e., neural networks performing worse at increasing depth), and capable of ensuring a good trade-off between convergence rapidity and expressivity/accuracy. Moreover, the high-level features extracted by the building blocks BB_2 and BB_4 are concatenated and used to feed the output layer of the model.

Finally, the `Output Layer` is instantiated with C neurons (one for each class) and equipped with a *softmax* activation function [5]. The proposed neural model is trained against a set $\mathcal{D} = \{(\mathbf{x}_1, \mathbf{y}_1), (\mathbf{x}_2, \mathbf{y}_2), \ldots, (\mathbf{x}_D, \mathbf{y}_D)\}$, where $\mathbf{x}_i$ is the matrix representation of the image and $\mathbf{y}$ is the class of the image. As regards the output, an one-hot encoding based on C classes is used to model the different labels each one indicating a specific malicious payloads. As it will be detailed later, in our work we considered C classes representing "clean" images and images cloaking JavaScript, HTML, PowerShell, Ethereum wallets, and URL/IP addresses. Finally, the training stage is responsible for optimizing the network weights by minimizing the loss function. The *categorical crossentropy* is adopted for the classification task and it is calculated as follows:

$$CCE(\mathbf{y}, \tilde{\mathbf{y}}) = - \sum_{i=1}^{|\mathcal{D}|} \mathbf{y}_i \log \tilde{\mathbf{y}}_i.$$

4.3   Ensembling via Soup Model

As discussed in Sect. 3, the proposed federated Algorithm 1 uses a soup model mechanism to merge the contribution of each model produced by the K peer nodes [26]. Basically, the underlying idea of this ensemble consists in performing an average of the DNN weights yielded by the peer model, per layer. This strategy

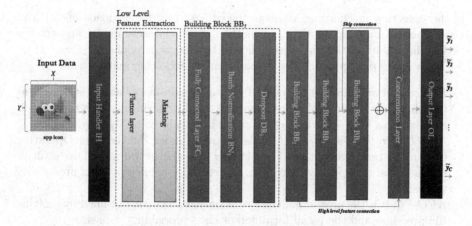

Fig. 4. Neural architecture for hidden content detection and classification.

has been named *Uniform Soup*. Formally, let be f(x, θ) a neural network with input data x and parameters $\theta \in \mathcal{R}^{\mathcal{D}}$. Let be $\theta = \texttt{FineTune}(\theta_0, \texttt{x})$ the parameters obtained by fine-tuning the pre-trained initialization θ_0 against data x. Let be $\theta_i = \texttt{FineTune}(\theta_0, \texttt{x}_\texttt{i})$ the parameters obtained by fine-tuning θ_0 against x_i, i.e., data of the node N_i. Model soup $f(x, \theta_T)$ is computed as an average θ_i, i.e., $\theta_T = \frac{1}{|K|} \sum_{i \in K} \theta_i$, where K is the number of peer nodes.

5   Experimental Results

To prove the effectiveness of our federated approach, we used the "Stego-Images-Dataset"[2] described in [1]. In essence, it is composed of $48,000$ icons of 512×512 pixels hiding different realistic malicious payloads, i.e., JavaScript, HTML, PowerShell, URLs, and Ethereum addresses, embedded via the LSB steganography technique. The payloads allow to model a wide-range of threats, such as malicious scripts and routines, links to additional configuration files or list of commands, and wallets collecting the outcome of cryptojacking and ransomware campaigns. The dataset is split into $16,000$, $8,000$, and $8,000$ icons, corresponding to the training, the validation and the test set. The training set is further divided among the server and the end nodes composing our architecture. In more detail, the 25% of the set ($4,000$ icons) is used to train the model on the server S, whereas the remaining 75% is assigned to the $K = 5$ end nodes, i.e., 15% images ($2,400$ icons) for each node. Instead, the validation set is used in its entirety to validate the ensemble model of the server and partially to validate the models of the end nodes. Finally, the dataset contains three different test sets (each one composed of $8,000$ icons) to model an attacker unaware/aware of the countermeasure and trying to elude the detection via obfuscation approaches. In particular, the first is generated considering "plain" payloads, i.e., the attacker is completely unaware

---

[2] https://www.kaggle.com/datasets/marcozuppelli/stegoimagesdataset.

of the detection mechanism, whereas the others consider payloads encoded in Base64 and compressed with a zip method. Such datasets model an attacker performing a sort of "lateral movement" to bypass security checks.

To evaluate our approach, we relied upon the following metrics[3]:

- *F1-Score*: it summarizes the overall system performances and it is defined as the harmonic mean of the precision and recall. Specifically, the precision is calculated as $\frac{TP}{TP+FP}$, whereas the recall is calculated as $\frac{TP}{TP+FN}$;
- *Area Under the Curve (AUC)*: it is the area under the Receiver Operating Characteristic curve, obtained by plotting the ratio between the false positive rate and the true positive rate (i.e., the recall) for different class probability values;
- *AUC-PR*: it is the area under the Precision-Recall curve, obtained by plotting the precision and the recall for different class probability values.

The first round of tests aimed at evaluating the effectiveness of our federated-learning-based approach in detecting malicious payloads hidden within images. Table 1 summarizes the obtained results and shows how the performance of the end nodes (i.e., peers) improves over 10 iterations of the algorithm. As reported, the average AUC of the end nodes improves from 94.3% in the 1-st iteration to a maximum value of 96.5% when the *max_iter* number of iterations defined in Algorithm 1 is reached. Also AUC-PR and F1-Score exhibit the same behavior: both metrics improve up to 82.9% and 81.1%, respectively. As a consequence, the performances of the server improve as well, i.e., from an AUC of 92.6% to 97.1%. A similar trend can be observed for the other metrics (the best values are reported in bold in Table 1). Such results demonstrate that federated learning can be effectively used to reveal the presence of concealed contents, while guaranteeing privacy and overcoming possible resource constraints.

The second round of tests aimed at comparing the federated approach against a "centralized" blueprint, i.e., when all the data are stored in the node S. Moreover, we also evaluated the different approaches when dealing with payloads obfuscated by the attacker, i.e., via Base64 encoding and zip compression. Table 2 showcases the results. Concerning plain and Base64-encoded payloads, the differences between the approaches are minimal. Instead, in the case of compressed zip payloads the federated solution achieves an improvement of ∼10% in terms of AUC and AUC-PR with respect to the centralized approach. Summing up, the main benefit in using the federated blueprint relies on the capability of the solution to achieve comparable performances with a fully centralized method without the necessity to move data in a single node. In this way, this peculiarity allows for using our approach also in scenarios in which the storage resources are limited, e.g., IoT ecosystems.

---

[3] TP is the number of positive cases correctly classified, FP is the number of negative cases incorrectly classified, FN is the number of positive cases incorrectly classified, and TN is the number of negative cases correctly classified.

Table 1. Performance of the federated approach.

Iteration	Model	AUC	AUC-PR	F1-Score
Initialization	*server*	0.926	0.745	0.699
1	*peer$_{avg}$*	0.943	0.775	0.737
	server	0.926	0.745	0.699
2	*peer$_{avg}$*	0.955	0.805	0.770
	server	**0.959**	**0.819**	**0.763**
3	*peer$_{avg}$*	0.955	0.804	0.768
	server	0.959	0.819	0.763
4	*peer$_{avg}$*	0.960	0.816	0.779
	server	0.959	0.819	0.763
5	*peer$_{avg}$*	0.960	0.816	0.782
	server	0.959	0.819	0.763
6	*peer$_{avg}$*	0.959	0.813	0.774
	server	0.959	0.819	0.763
7	*peer$_{avg}$*	0.960	0.820	0.783
	server	**0.962**	**0.826**	0.641
8	*peer$_{avg}$*	0.965	0.829	0.797
	server	**0.971**	**0.845**	0.744
9	*peer$_{avg}$*	0.959	0.818	0.783
	server	0.971	0.845	0.744
10	*peer$_{avg}$*	0.965	0.829	0.811
	server	0.970	0.842	**0.817**

Table 2. Comparison between centralized and federated approaches against different test sets.

Approach	Coding	AUC	AUC-PR	F1-Score
Centralized	Plain	**0.972**	**0.851**	**0.835**
	Base64	**0.899**	**0.605**	0.589
	zip	0.776	0.397	0.344
Federated	Plain	0.970	0.842	0.817
	Base64	0.893	0.594	**0.614**
	zip	**0.856**	**0.498**	**0.363**

6   Conclusions and Future Works

In this paper we have presented a federated framework for the detection of malicious assets cloaked within images of applications delivered through stores. Results showcased the effectiveness of the approach, which can lead to performances similar to those achieved via centralized solutions. Yet, a federated mechanism could be able to prevent constraints and bottlenecks characterizing single-point blueprints, e.g., scalability issues and lack of comprehensive snapshots for training the models.

Future work aims at extending our approach to detect different steganographic threats, including malware hiding data in network traffic or in other multimedia carriers. Moreover, part of our ongoing research is devoted to make the overall idea more general and not only limited to the case of stores. Specifically, we are working towards an edge-based architecture with nodes placed at the border of the network cooperating to detect/classify Internet-wide threats.

References

1. Cassavia, N., Caviglione, L., Guarascio, M., Manco, G., Zuppelli, M.: Detection of steganographic threats targeting digital images in heterogeneous ecosystems through machine learning. J. Wirel. Mob. Netw. Ubiquit. Comput. Dependable Appl. **13**, 50–67 (2022)
2. Caviglione, L., Mazurczyk, W.: Never mind the malware, here's the stegomalware. IEEE Securi. Priv. **20**(5), 101–106 (2022)
3. Cheddad, A., Condell, J., Curran, K., Mc Kevitt, P.: Digital image steganography: survey and analysis of current methods. Signal Process. **90**(3), 727–752 (2010)
4. Gibert, D., Mateu, C., Planes, J.: The rise of machine learning for detection and classification of malware: research developments, trends and challenges. J. Netw. Comput. Appl. **153**, 102526 (2020)
5. Guarascio, M., Manco, G., Ritacco, E.: Deep learning. Encycl. Bioinform. Comput. Biol.: ABC Bioinform. **1–3**, 634–647 (2018)
6. Guarascio, M., Zuppelli, M., Cassavia, N., Caviglione, L., Manco, G.: Revealing MageCart-like threats in favicons via artificial intelligence. In: Proceedings of the 17th International Conference on Availability, Reliability and Security, pp. 1–7 (2022)
7. He, D., Chan, S., Guizani, M.: Mobile application security: malware threats and defenses. IEEE Wirel. Commun. **22**(1), 138–144 (2015)
8. He, K., Zhang, X., Ren, S., Sun, J.: Deep residual learning for image recognition. In: Proceedings of the IEEE Conference on Computer Vision and Pattern Recognition (CVPR), pp. 770–778 (2016)
9. Hinton, G.E., Srivastava, N., Krizhevsky, A., Sutskever, I., Salakhutdinov, R.: Dropout: a simple way to prevent neural networks from overfitting. J. Mach. Learn. Res. **15**, 1929–1958 (2014)
10. Hinton, G.E., Srivastava, N., Krizhevsky, A., Sutskever, I., Salakhutdinov, R.R.: Improving neural networks by preventing co-adaptation of feature detectors. arXiv preprint arXiv:1207.0580 (2012)
11. Hsu, R.H., et al.: A privacy-preserving federated learning system for Android malware detection based on edge computing. In: 15th Asia Joint Conference on Information Security (AsiaJCIS), pp. 128–136. IEEE (2020)
12. Jiang, C., Yin, K., Xia, C., Huang, W.: FedHGCDroid: an adaptive multidimensional federated learning for privacy-preserving Android malware classification. Entropy **24**(7), 919 (2022)

13. Lin, K.Y., Huang, W.R.: Using federated learning on malware classification. In: 2020 22nd International Conference on Advanced Communication Technology (ICACT), pp. 585–589. IEEE (2020)
14. Mazurczyk, W., Caviglione, L.: Information hiding as a challenge for malware detection. IEEE Secur. Priv. **13**(2), 89–93 (2015)
15. Monika, A., Eswari, R.: Prevention of hidden information security attacks by neutralizing stego-malware. Comput. Electr. Eng. **101**, 107990 (2022)
16. Mylonas, A., Kastania, A., Gritzalis, D.: Delegate the smartphone user? Security awareness in smartphone platforms. Comput. Secur. **34**, 47–66 (2013)
17. Nair, V., Hinton, G.E.: Rectified linear units improve restricted Boltzmann machines. In: Proceedings of the 27th International Conference on International Conference on Machine Learning (ICML), Haifa, Israel, pp. 807–814 (2010)
18. Oz, H., Aris, A., Levi, A., Uluagac, A.S.: A survey on ransomware: evolution, taxonomy, and defense solutions. ACM Comput. Surv. **54**(11s), 1–37 (2022)
19. Papageorgiou, A., Strigkos, M., Politou, E., Alepis, E., Solanas, A., Patsakis, C.: Security and privacy analysis of mobile health applications: the alarming state of practice. IEEE Access **6**, 9390–9403 (2018)
20. Pawlicka, A., Jaroszewska-Choras, D., Choras, M., Pawlicki, M.: Guidelines for stego/malware detection tools: achieving GDPR compliance. IEEE Technol. Soc. Mag. **39**(4), 60–70 (2020)
21. Rahman, S.A., Tout, H., Talhi, C., Mourad, A.: Internet of things intrusion detection: centralized, on-device, or federated learning? IEEE Netw. **34**(6), 310–317 (2020)
22. Shamili, A.S., Bauckhage, C., Alpcan, T.: Malware detection on mobile devices using distributed machine learning. In: 20th International Conference on Pattern Recognition, pp. 4348–4351. IEEE (2010)
23. Suarez-Tangil, G., Tapiador, J.E., Peris-Lopez, P.: Stegomalware: playing hide and seek with malicious components in smartphone apps. In: Lin, D., Yung, M., Zhou, J. (eds.) Inscrypt 2014. LNCS, vol. 8957, pp. 496–515. Springer, Cham (2015). https://doi.org/10.1007/978-3-319-16745-9_27
24. Tian, P., Chen, Z., Yu, W., Liao, W.: Towards asynchronous federated learning based threat detection: a DC-Adam approach. Comput. Secur. **108**, 102344 (2021)
25. Wang, H., Li, H., Guo, Y.: Understanding the evolution of mobile app ecosystems: a longitudinal measurement study of Google Play. In: The World Wide Web conference, pp. 1988–1999 (2019)
26. Wortsman, M., et al.: Model soups: averaging weights of multiple fine-tuned models improves accuracy without increasing inference time. In: Chaudhuri, K., Jegelka, S., Song, L., Szepesvari, C., Niu, G., Sabato, S. (eds.) Proceedings of the 39th International Conference on Machine Learning, vol. 162, pp. 23965–23998. PMLR (2022)
27. Yang, H., He, H., Zhang, W., Cao, X.: FedSteg: a federated transfer learning framework for secure image steganalysis. IEEE Trans. Netw. Sci. Eng. **8**(2), 1084–1094 (2020)
28. Yuan, Z., Lu, Y., Xue, Y.: DroidDetector: Android malware characterization and detection using deep learning. Tsinghua Sci. Technol. **21**(1), 114–123 (2016)
29. Zhou, W., Zhou, Y., Jiang, X., Ning, P.: Detecting repackaged smartphone applications in third-party android marketplaces. In: Proceedings of the Second ACM Conference on Data and Application Security and Privacy, pp. 317–326 (2012)
30. Zuppelli, M., Manco, G., Caviglione, L., Guarascio, M.: Sanitization of images containing stegomalware via machine learning approaches. In: Proceedings of the Italian Conference on Cybersecurity (ITASEC), vol. 2940, pp. 374–386 (2021)

Machine Learning and Network Traffic to Distinguish Between Malware and Benign Applications

Laith Abualigah[1,2,3,4,5]([✉]), Sayel Abualigah[6], Mothanna Almahmoud[6], Agostino Forestiero[7], Gagan Sachdeva[8], and Essam S. Hanandeh[9]

[1] Hourani Center for Applied Scientific Research, Al-Ahliyya Amman University, Amman, Jordan
aligah.2020@gmail.com
[2] Faculty of Information Technology, Middle East University, Amman, Jordan
[3] Applied Science Research Center, Applied Science Private University, Amman, Jordan
[4] School of Computer Sciences, Universiti Sains Malaysia, George Town, Pulau Pinang, Malaysia
[5] Computer Science Department, Prince Hussein Bin Abdullah, Faculty for Information Technology, Al Al-Bayt University, Mafraq 25113, Jordan
[6] Department of Computer Information Systems, Jordan University of Science and Technology, Ar-Ramtha, Jordan
[7] Performance Computing and Networking, National Research Council of Italy, 87036 Rende, Italy
agostino.forestiero@icar.cnr.it
[8] First Abu Dhabi Bank, Abu Dhabi, UAE
[9] Department of Computer Information System, Zarqa University, Zarqa, Jordan
hanandeh@zu.edu.jo

Abstract. Virus detection software is widely used for servers, systems, and devices that seek to maintain security and reliability. Although these programs provide an excellent safety level, the traditional defense methods fail to detect new Malware. The more advanced approach relies on predicting malicious behavior with dynamic analysis of the process executed. This paper presents a new method for detecting malware using machine learning algorithms applied to data obtained from the Cuckoo sandbox. The Cuckoo sandbox isolates the file being analyzed, providing detailed dynamic analysis reports. The machine learning algorithms were compared and the most important features were identified. The results were obtained using six popular classifiers, including SVM, Random Forest, and LightGBM, and the XGBOOST algorithm had the highest accuracy, at an average of 97%. However, the research on machine learning-based malware analysis is limited in terms of computational complexity and detection accuracy.

Keywords: Machine Learning · XGBOOST · Malware · Network Traffic · Classification

© ICST Institute for Computer Sciences, Social Informatics and Telecommunications Engineering 2023
Published by Springer Nature Switzerland AG 2023. All Rights Reserved
C. Comito and D. Talia (Eds.): PerSOM 2022, LNICST 494, pp. 96–108, 2023.
https://doi.org/10.1007/978-3-031-31469-8_7

1 Introduction

Malware with particular types is one of the most common viruses studied in the last years in dynamic or static environments using various processing algorithms [1]. The detection of viruses such as Malware, spyware, or other complex tasks for a person or device to deal with in dynamic or static environments because the nature of these viruses is difficult to understand easily [2]. The continuous growth of Malware generates various information and security threats [3, 4].

A malware virus is a malicious program that some users create on our devices to obtain personal information, destroy programs on the devices, or obtain financial gain [5]. Many types of malware files exist, such as dynamic-link libraries (DLLs), executable files, or assembly-level instructions [6]. Therefore, it is essential to discover this type of virus, it can detect some types through the set of powers that it requires or through the behavior that it follows, but the method of detecting new types of viruses using this method may not be safe and accurate to a large extent, so the implementation of these applications. A dynamic environment in different operating systems, such as the cloud environment and the virtual machine (for example, VMware, sandbox), enables us to understand the nature of these programs and our ability to quickly and accurately detect them and identify malicious programs from them [7, 8].

Android, being one of the most widely used mobile operating systems in the world, has become a target for malware attacks due to its open-source code and the ability to install third-party applications without central control. Researchers and developers have been working on various security solutions, including static analysis, dynamic analysis, artificial intelligence, and data science to improve cybersecurity. Advancements in these fields have greatly improved the ability to predict malicious activities by using analytical models based on data. The goal of this research is to extract features for building prediction models using both static and dynamic analysis techniques.

Machine learning algorithms are widely used in detecting malicious programs, and they have proven accurate and high- speed results. In this paper, machine learning algorithms were used, and six of the most powerful classifiers were chosen to implement and build the system on them: Support vector machine (SVM), Random Forest, LightGBM, Decision Tree, k-nearest neighbors (KNN), and Extreme Gradient Boosting (XGBoost). Where the data set is entered on these algorithms and a particular model is built for each one to reach the highest Accuracy and results, the comparison between them and the most influential features are also determined.

This paper's reminder is organized as follows: Sect. 2 presents the previous related work on malware detection. Section 3 describes the proposed methodology used. Section 4 discusses the data analysis and experimental results. The conclusion of this paper is explained in Sect. 5.

2 Literature Review

Many researchers in previous work study virus detection in a dynamic environment using machine learning algorithms. This paper focuses on malware detection in a dynamic environment using machine learning algorithms.

Poudyal et al. in [6] used machine learning algorithms to detect malware from assembly level instructions and dynamic link libraries (DLLs) and determine if the sample is a ransomware virus. The dataset used in this study consisted of 302 samples of malware from various sources including Virus Total, Virus Share, and the open-source malware repository, the zoo. The algorithms used were Bayesian Network (BN), Logistic Regression, and Sequential Minimal Optimization with Linear Kernel (SMO with LK), SMO with Poly kernel (PK), J48, Random Forest (RF), AdaboostM1 with J48, and AdaboostM1 with RF. Seven evaluation metrics were used to assess the algorithms: True positive rate (TPR), false positive rate (FPR), precision, recall, f-measure, and accuracy. The results showed that AdaboostM1 with RF had the highest accuracy for assembly level instructions (ASI) and DLLs at 97.8916% and 90.8012% respectively. For both assembly level instructions and DLLs, Random Forest (RF) had the best accuracy of 97.9532%.

Niveditha et al. in [9] proposed a framework where dynamic and static malware detection techniques are efficiently combined to classify and identify Malware at day zero with High Accuracy. The framework was tested and estimated on a sample of large data files from 0.1 million files, including clean files, to 0.03. It contains a variety of malware families in 0.13 million malicious binary files. Results showed that SVM had the best Accuracy of 93.03% for detecting Malware and benign species using $10\times$ cross-validation. The proposed framework was intended to resolve issues and concerns about identifying zero-day Malware early.

Rabadi et al. in [10] proposed a new method for detecting and classifying malware using API-based dynamic feature extraction. This approach analyzes API calls and their arguments using machine learning algorithms. Two methods were designed for this purpose: the first method treats the complete list of arguments for each API call as a single feature, while the second method treats each argument for each API call separately as a single feature. To test its accuracy, they used datasets of 7,774 benign samples and 7,105 malicious samples of ten different types of malware. The results showed that their classification module had an accuracy of 98.0253%, and the malware detection module had an accuracy of more than 99.8992%, outperforming many existing API-based malware detection techniques.

Singh et al. in [11] conducted an analysis of seven techniques that use API calls for malware detection. They developed and evaluated the effectiveness of basic parameters of simple and advanced classification algorithms to improve the binary classification of binary files into benign or malicious programs. Dynamic API calls were used in the training of classifiers. Machine learning (ML) parameter tuning was performed to improve the accuracy of binary classification of binary files into malware or benign. Basic parameters such as k-value, kernel function, tree depth, loss function, partition criteria, learning rate, and number of capabilities were evaluated using API calls. They then evaluated the tuned machine learning algorithms using 6,434 benign and 8,634 malware samples. The results showed that Random Forest produced the highest accuracy of 99.1% in binary classification.

Kumar et al. in [12] used a methodology involving the combination of Fuzzy AHP and Fuzzy TOPSIS technology to assess the impact of different malware analysis techniques on a web application perspective. This study used different versions of the University's web application to assess the impact of many current malware analysis technologies. The study shows that reverse engineering is the most effective method for analyzing complex Malware. Zhang et al. in [13] presented machine learning algorithms to detect the particular type of malware virus from eight ransomware families (cryptolocker, cryptowall, Cryrar, locky, petya, reveton, teslacrypt, and wannacry). There are 1787 ransomware samples that the authors used to detect if the sample is ransomware or not. After collecting the dataset, they extracted the features using Term Frequency-Inverse document frequency (TF-IDF) and n-gram. Naïve Bayes, Decision Tree, random forest, K-Nearest Neighbor, and Gradient Boosting Decision Tree are machine learning algorithms. The results shown that the random forest gave the best Accuracy of 91.43% when using the value of n-gram is 3.

Singh et al. in [14] applied machine learning algorithms to detect one of the most famous viruses (Malware) in the dynamic analysis environment, called Cuckoo sandbox. They collected datasets about Malware from VirusShare (8524 malware samples) and VirusTotal (7239 malware samples) Malware dataset. The K-Nearest Neighbor, Naïve Bayes, Support Vector Machine, Decision Tree, random forest, Gradient Boosting, and AdaBoost. Are machine learning algorithms. They have shown that the AdaBoost obtained the best accuracy value of 0.9863 compared with the others.

Alzaylaee et al. in [15] proposed machine learning algorithms to detect Malware in the Android operating system. The dataset was collected from 2,444 Android applications; half of it is malware samples and 49 families of the Android malware genome project. The authors used machine learning algorithms are Support Vector Machine, Naive Bayes, Simple Logistic, Multilayer Perceptron, Partial Decision Trees, Random Forest, and J48 Decision Tree. They have shown that the RF achieved the best results in detecting malware from Malware from Android applications, around 0.931.

Kilgallon et al. in [16] proposed two techniques to predict the required time in malware detection in the sandbox and to classify the sample if it is Malware or not. The authors used machine learning algorithms in the first problem while using a novel approach in the second. The dataset used is about 3,320 malware samples for two problems. The classification algorithms applied in their experiments are Decision Tree, Random Forest, Support Vector Machine, Neural Network, and K-nearest Neighbors. The results in the classification problem show that the Neural Network gave the best Accuracy with 92.18%. While the Accuracy of prediction required time problem is equal to 90%.

Kumar et al. in [17] proposed a machine learning model to detect the malware threat in a cloud environment called a clustering model. They collected malware files (1344 files) and cleaning files (1436 files) from VirusShare and VirusTotal sites. The malware files contain many malware types like rootkit, adware, spyware, virus, Trojan, worm, backdoor, and hijacker. While the cleaning files contain PDF, PHP, and other clean files. The clustering model obtained the 95.7% as an accuracy values in detection process, where the number of clusters is 18 and the threshold value is 150. Other related machine learning methods can be found in [18–25]. Table 1 shows the summarization of these works.

Table 1. Related work

Ref	Year	Algorithm used	Dataset used	Dataset size	Results
[12]	2017	Support Vector Machine, Naive Bayes, Simple Logistic, Multilayer Perceptron, Partial Decision Trees	Android application	2,444 applications	The true positive rate of Random Forest gave = 0.931
[13]	2017	Decision Tree, Random Forest, Support Vector Machine, Neural Network, and K-nearest Neighbors	Malware detection dataset	3,320 samples	Accuracy of Neural Network in classification problem = 92.18%. While in the accuracy of prediction required time = 90%
[15]	2019	Proposed own network approach	They used four malware datasets: 1- Malgenome and Contagio 2- VirusShare site 3- Playdrone 4- Google Play store	1- 1.2k and 0.3k samples 2- 24k apps 3- 22k apps 4- 1.2k benign apps	Accuracy = 0.94
[16]	2019	• Random Forest • Logistic Regression • Naïve Bayes • Stochastic Gradient Descent • K-Nearest Neighbors • Support Vector Machine	They used three datasets: benign, ransomware, and malware files	300 benign files 1000 ransomware samples 900 malware samples	Accuracy of Random Forest = 99.53%

(*continued*)

Table 1. (*continued*)

Ref	Year	Algorithm used	Dataset used	Dataset size	Results
[17]	2019	Logistic regression Decision Tree Random Forest Bagging Classifier AdaBoost Classifier Tree Classifier Gradient Classifier	They used benign and malware files	800 benign files and 2200 malware files	Accuracy of Gradient Classifier = 94.64%
[5]	2019	BN, Logistic Regression, SMO with LK, SMO with PK, J48, RF, AdaboostM1 with J48, and AdaboostM1 with RF	Malware dataset from virus resources	302 samples	Accuracy of AdaboostM1 with RF = 97.8916%, 90.8012% in ASI, DLLs, respectively Accuracy of RF = 97.9532% in both ASI, DLLs datasets
[14]	2020	Clustering model	Malware dataset from VirusShare and VirusTotal sites	2780 sample files	Accuracy = 95.7%
[10]	2020	Naïve Bayes, Decision Tree, random forest, K-Nearest Neighbor, and Gradient Boosting Decision Tree	Ransomware dataset	1787 samples	Accuracy of Random forest = 91.43%
[11]	2020	K-Nearest Neighbor, Naïve Bayes, Support Vector Machine, Decision Tree, random forest, Gradient Boosting, and AdaBoost	Two sores dataset: VirusShare and VirusTotal	8524 and 7239 samples	AdaBoost obtained the best accuracy value of 0.9863

3 The Proposed Method

This paper proposes a method for detecting Malware that relies on machine learning algorithms. Figure 1 illustrates the overall process for our proposed method. After cleaning and manipulating the data, a discovery model is constructed using six machine learning algorithms to classify unknown binary samples into Malware or benign files. Then a set of evaluation procedures is used to determine and compare each model's Accuracy.

Figure 1 shows the system architecture of the proposed methodology used in this paper. The following section explains the components of the system architecture.

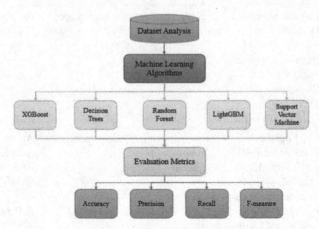

Fig. 1. System Architecture

3.1 Description of Churn Dataset

The dataset used was extracted by Urcuqui and Christian. And Navarro and Andres. (2016), where the data was obtained by creating a binary vector of the permissions used for each application analyzed (1 = used, 0 = unused). The malware/benign samples were then divided by "type". 1 malware and 0 non-malware. The authors note that an essential topic of work is building a good variety of Malware.

Data extracted from the Android Genome Project (MalGenome), an active dataset from 2012 through the end of 2015, this batch of Malware has a size of 1,260 apps, aggregated into a total of 49 families. A batch of pcap files from the integrated Droid-Collector project was used by 4705 benign and 7846 malicious applications. A particular script processed all files to extract the features, and this analysis aims to know the possibility of distinguishing between Malware and benign applications using network traffic (Table 2).

3.2 Data Analysis

One critical stage is data cleaning and processing, and we searched for existing data to find 7845 missing data in duration, avg_local_pkt_rate, and avg_remote_pkt_rate. The ideal solution in a situation like this is to delete these features. Since most of the data we have is digital, it was essential to extract the statistical analysis of these features to understand the data deeply, and we concluded that the best network features are:

- (R1): TCP packets refer to the number of packets sent and received during TCP communication.

Table 2. Features of dataset

Type	Features
Categorical Features	name
	Type
Numerical Features	dist_port_tcp
	external_ips
	vulume_bytes
	udp_packets
	tcp_urg_packet
	source_app_packets
	remote_app_packets
	source_app_bytes
	remote_app_bytes
	duracion
	avg_local_pkt_rate
	avg_remote_pkt_rate
	source_app_packets.1
	dns_query_times
	tcp_packets

- (R2): Different TCP packets represent the total number of packets that are different from TCP.
- (R3): External IP denotes the number of external addresses that the application attempted to communicate with.
- (R4): Volume of bytes refers to the number of bytes sent from the application to external sites.
- (R5): UDP packets, represent the total number of packets transmitted via UDP during communication.
- (R6): Packets of the source application, refer to the number of packets sent from the application to a remote server.
- (R7): Remote application packages, indicate the number of packages received from external sources.
- (R8): Bytes of the application source, represent the volume (in bytes) of communication between the application and the server.
- (R9): Bytes of the application remote, refer to the volume (in bytes) of data sent from the server to the emulator.
- (R10): DNS queries, refer to the number of DNS requests.

3.3 Machine Learning Methods

Extreme Gradient Boosting (XGBoost) is one of the most powerful and effective grading algorithms in the last few years and is the one that will be used to predict the class label. XGBoost performance was tested and compared with various popular classification techniques.

- First: The data set is used in two parts. The first part will be used for tuning, while the second will train and test the developed models. Stratified sampling is used because the data set is not balanced, and they must have the same share of category labels in both segment samples.
- Second: XGBoost parameters are set. This step helps greatly improve the classifier's performance and maximize it over the rest of the experiments. The second part of the dataset is used to test and test the algorithm with a 10-fold validation technique. In this way, nine folds are used to train the pattern, and 1fold is used to test the pattern. This process is repeated 10 times. Then the results are averaged.
- Third: XGBoost was trained using redundant sample data and tested on non-exhaustive test data.
- Fourth: XGBoost performance is evaluated using standard rating scales: Accuracy, recall, and F1.
- Fifthly, other classifiers such as Decision Trees (DT), Random Forest, LightGBM, and Support Vector Machine (SVM) are used, and compare their results with XGBOOST.

3.4 Evaluation Measure

To evaluate XGBoost, selectors, and classifiers in Label Prediction, the performance criteria for Accuracy, recall, precision, and F-measure are used. Binary performance evaluation criteria are calculated based on the confusion matrix. The false positive and positive current states are referred to as FP and TP, while the false negative and true negative states are abbreviated as FN and TN, as shown in Table 3.

Table 3. Confusion matrix of class label

		Production Class	
		0	1
Actual Class	0	TP	FP
	1	FN	FP

The precision is the percentage of correctly predicted student labels. It is computed using the following equation

$$Precision = \frac{TP}{TP + FP}$$

Recall expresses the percentage of the correctly predicted student label. It is calculated using the equation.

$$Recall = \frac{TP}{TP + FN}$$

Accuracy represents the percentage of the sum of correct predictions. The following equation gives it:

In this stage, the prediction model is built and tested with the following steps:

$$Accuracy = \frac{TP + TN}{TP + FP + TN + FN}$$

Neither recall nor Accuracy alone can describe a classifier's efficiency because good performance according to one of these indicators does not necessarily mean good performance according to the other. For this reason, the F- measure, a common combination of these two measures, is used as one metric to evaluate classifier performance. This measure is defined as the harmonic mean of recall and Accuracy and is calculated using the following equation.

$$F - meadure = \frac{2 * Precision * Recall}{Precision * Recall}$$

4 Experiments and Results

Our proposed method detects malware applications and distinguishes them from benign ones. We conducted several experiments to show the efficacy and Accuracy of the classifiers used.

The six algorithms chosen in this paper are representative and widely used for binary classification. However, in this research, we aim to classify Malware and good ware into two categories (0 and 1). We chose the following six algorithms for our experiments:

Random Forest (RF) is an ensemble learning technique that can be used for regression, classification, and feature importance analysis. It produces results by combining the outputs of multiple decision trees that are created through training processes.

K-Nearest Neighbors (KNN) is a machine learning algorithm that can be used for both classification and regression. It utilizes a pattern recognition approach to classify an element by determining the class of the K closest elements in the training dataset.

Support Vector Machine (SVM) is a widely used supervised learning model for pattern recognition and data analysis. It generates a non-probabilistic binary linear classification model that classifies new data based on which class it belongs to.

LightGBM is a scalable and efficient tree-based learning framework. It has been utilized for various reasons, including faster training speed, higher performance, lower memory usage, improved accuracy, support for parallel and GPU-based learning, and the ability to process large-scale data.

The results showed a clear advantage for XGBOOTS compared to the rest of the classifications used, which achieved an accuracy of 96.6%, followed by LightGBM with an accuracy of 93.3%, and was the least accurate for Random Forest, achieving only 72.25% (Table 4).

Table 4. Model accuracy

Model	Accuracy
XGBoost	96.697310
LightGBM	93.309499
KNN	87.742996
Decision Tree	87.420192
SVM	75.188203
Random Forest	72.259148

Since the data was not balanced, we worked to increase the model's Accuracy by working to control the data balance. SMOTE was used to obtain balanced data and thus better Accuracy. The Accuracy of XGBOOTS has reached 99%, and the Accuracy of the rest of the classifiers has also increased, except for SVM, where it was not affected, and the results of its Accuracy as it appeared in the first experiment remained 75.1% (Table 5).

Table 5. The accuracy results after SMOTE

Model	Accuracy
XGBoost	99.061967
LightGBM	93.348493
KNN	89.906080
Decision Tree	89.226396
Random Forest	77.948591
SVM	75.642610

5 Conclusion

Malware detection is one of the critical topics that the world cares about today. The great advances in machine learning and artificial intelligence have accelerated and greatly advanced malware detection. The types of malicious programs and applications are detected in two ways, static and dynamic. In this research, a set of machine learning algorithms are applied to data extracted from applications that have been implemented and features extracted from them in a virtual work environment, and six classifiers were used: DT, random forest, LightGBM, KNN, SVM, and XGBOOST were applied. The highest Accuracy for XGBOOST was 97%, followed by LightGBM at 93.309499%, then KNN at 87.742996%, and the lowest was Random Forest at 72.259148%. To increase the Accuracy of the classifier, the data was converted into balanced data because it was not unbalanced, and it was re-model to increase the Accuracy of the data.

References

1. Ye, Y., Li, T., Adjeroh, D., Iyengar, S.S.: A survey on malware detection using data mining techniques. ACM Comput. Surv. **50**(3), 1–40 (2017)
2. Jerlin, M.A., Marimuthu, K.: A new malware detection system using machine learning techniques for API call sequences. J. Appl. Secur. Res. **13**(1), 45–62 (2018)
3. Biondi, F., Given-Wilson, T., Legay, A., Puodzius, C., Quilbeuf, J.: Tutorial: an overview of malware detection and evasion techniques. In: Margaria, T., Steffen, B. (eds.) ISoLA 2018. LNCS, vol. 11244, pp. 565–586. Springer, Cham (2018). https://doi.org/10.1007/978-3-030-03418-4_34
4. Poudyal, S., Subedi, K.P., Dasgupta, D.: A framework for analyzing ransomware using machine learning. In: Proceedings of the 2018 IEEE Symposium Series on Computational Intelligence SSCI, January 2018, pp. 1692–1699 (2019)
5. Vurdelja, I., Blažić, I., Drašković, D., Nikolić, B.: Detection of Linux Malware Using System Tracers – An Overview of Solutions, pp. 1–6 (2020)
6. Niveditha, V.R., Ananthan, T.V., Amudha, S., Sam, D., Srinidhi, S.: Detect and classify zero day malware efficiently in big data platform. Int. J. Adv. Sci. Technol. **29**(4) Special Issue, 1947–1954 (2020)
7. Rabadi, D., Teo, S.G.: Advanced windows methods on malware detection and classification, pp. 54–68 (2020)
8. Singh, J., Singh, J.: Assessment of supervised machine learning algorithms using dynamic API calls for malware detection. Int. J. Comput. Appl. 1–8 (2020)
9. Kumar, R., Alenezi, M., Ansari, M., Gupta, B., Agrawal, A., Khan, R.: Evaluating the impact of malware analysis techniques for securing web applications through a decision-making framework under fuzzy environment. Int. J. Intell. Eng. Syst. **13**(6), 94–109 (2020)
10. Zhang, H., Xiao, X., Mercaldo, F., Ni, S., Martinelli, F., Sangaiah, A.K.: Classification of ransomware families with machine learning based on N-gram of opcodes. Future Gener. Comput. Syst. **90**, 211–221 (2019)
11. Singh, J., Singh, J.: Detection of malicious software by analyzing the behavioral artifacts using machine learning algorithms. Inf. Softw. Technol. **121**, 106273 (2020)
12. Alzaylaee, M.K., Yerima, S.Y., Sezer, S.: Emulator vs real phone: android malware detection using machine learning. In: IWSPA 2017 – Proceedings of the 3rd ACM International Workshop on Security and Privacy Analytics co-located with CODASPY 2017, pp. 65–72 (2017)
13. Kilgallon, S., De La Rosa, L., Cavazos, J.: Improving the effectiveness and efficiency of dynamic malware analysis with machine learning. In: Proceedings of the - 2017 Resilience Week, RWS 2017, pp. 30–36 (2017)

14. Kumar, R., Sethi, K., Prajapati, N., Rout, R.R., Bera, P.: Machine learning based malware detection in cloud environment using clustering approach. In: 2020 11th International Conference on Computing, Communication and Networking Technologies ICCCNT 2020 (2020)

15. Krüger, F.: Activity, context, and plan recognition with computational causal behaviour models. ResearchGate (2018)

16. Al-Shatnwai, A.M., Faris, M.: Predicting customer retention using XGBoost and balancing methods. Int. J. Adv. Comput. Sci. Appl. **11**(7), 704–712 (2020)

17. Vafeiadis, T., Diamantaras, K.I., Sarigiannidis, G., Chatzisavvas, K.C.: A comparison of machine learning techniques for customer churn prediction. Simul. Model. Pract. Theor. **55**, 1–9 (2015)

18. Gul, F., et al.: A centralized strategy for multi-agent exploration. IEEE Access **10**, 126871–126884 (2022)

19. Abualigah, L., Elaziz, M.A., Khodadadi, N., Forestiero, A., Jia, H., Gandomi, A.H. Aquila optimizer based pso swarm intelligence for IoT task scheduling application in cloud computing. In: Houssein, E.H., Abd Elaziz, M., Oliva, D., Abualigah, L. (eds.) Integrating Meta-Heuristics and Machine Learning for Real-World Optimization Problems. Studies in Computational Intelligence, vol. 1038, pp. 481–497. Springer, Cham (2022). https://doi.org/10.1007/978-3-030-99079-4_19

20. Abualigah, L., Forestiero, A., Elaziz, M.A.: Bio-inspired agents for a distributed NLP-based clustering in smart environments. In: Abraham, A., et al. (eds.) SoCPaR 2021. LNNS, vol. 417, pp. 678–687. Springer, Cham (2022). https://doi.org/10.1007/978-3-030-96302-6_64

21. Alzu'bi, D., et al.: Kidney tumor detection and classification based on deep learning approaches: a new dataset in CT scans. J. Healthc. Eng. (2022)

22. Khazalah, A., et al.: Image processing identification for sapodilla using convolution neural network (cnn) and transfer learning techniques. In: Abualigah, L. (eds.) Classification Applications with Deep Learning and Machine Learning Technologies. Studies in Computational Intelligence, vol. 1071, pp. 107–127. Springer, Cham (2023). https://doi.org/10.1007/978-3-031-17576-3_5

23. Melhem, M.K.B., Abualigah, L., Zitar, R.A., Hussien, A.G., Oliva, D.: Comparative study on Arabic text classification: challenges and opportunities. In: Abualigah, L. (eds.) Classification Applications with Deep Learning and Machine Learning Technologies. Studies in Computational Intelligence, vol. 1071, pp. 217–224. Springer, Cham (2023). https://doi.org/10.1007/978-3-031-17576-3_10

24. Anuar, N.A., et al.: Rambutan image classification using various deep learning approaches. In: Abualigah, L. (eds.) Classification Applications with Deep Learning and Machine Learning Technologies. Studies in Computational Intelligence, vol. 1071, pp. 23–43. Springer, Cham (2023). https://doi.org/10.1007/978-3-031-17576-3_2

25. Ke, C., et al.: Mango varieties classification-based optimization with transfer learning and deep learning approaches. In: Abualigah, L. (eds.) Classification Applications with Deep Learning and Machine Learning Technologies. Studies in Computational Intelligence, vol. 1071, pp. 45–65. Springer, Cham (2023). https://doi.org/10.1007/978-3-031-17576-3_3

Emerging Applications

A Comparative Study of the Coulomb's and Franklin's Laws Inspired Algorithm (CFA) with Modern Evolutionary Algorithms for Numerical Optimization

Mojtaba Ghasemi[1], Mohsen Zare[2], Amir Zahedi[3], Rasul Hemmati[4], Laith Abualigah[5,6,7,8,9]([✉]), and Agostino Forestiero[10]

[1] Department of Electronics and Electrical Engineering, Shiraz University of Technology, Shiraz, Iran

[2] Department of Electrical Engineering, Faculty of Engineering, Jahrom University, Jahrom, Fras, Iran

[3] Department of Electrical and Computer Engineering, Tarbiat Modares University, Tehran, Iran

[4] Department of Electrical and Computer Engineering, Marquette University, Milwaukee, Wisconsin, USA

[5] Hourani Center for Applied Scientific Research, Al-Ahliyya Amman University, Amman, Jordan

[6] Faculty of Information Technology, Middle East University, Amman 11831, Jordan

[7] Applied Science Research Center, Applied Science Private University, Amman 11931, Jordan

[8] School of Computer Sciences, Universiti Sains Malaysia, 11800 George Town, Pulau Pinang, Malaysia

[9] Computer Science Department, Prince Hussein Bin Abdullah Faculty for Information Technology, Al Al-Bayt University, Mafraq 25113, Jordan

[10] Institute for High Performance Computing and Networking, National Research Council of Italy, Rende, Italy

Abstract. Coulomb and Franklin's electricity laws are used in this paper to model an efficient optimization algorithm based on electric particle searches, which has been named CFA. For the CFA optimizer, the influence of electrically charged particles on each other in charged things has been predicated on the forces of attraction and repulsion. Evolutionary algorithms (EA) such as hybrid real coded genetic algorithm (RCGA) which combines the global and local search (GL-25), differential evolution (DE) with strategy adaptation (SaDE), composite DE (CoDE), the improved standard particle swarm optimization 2011 (SPSO2013) and the grouped comprehensive learning PSO (GCLPSO) are compared to the CFA optimizer for finding global solutions of seven basic benchmark functions of high dimension D = 50. (GCLPSO). Experiments have shown that the suggested CFA optimizer is quite effective and competitive for the benchmark functions. Note that the source code of the CFA algorithm is publicly available at https://www.optim-app.com/projects/cfa, https://www.mathworks.com/matlabcentral/fileexchange/127727-franklin-s-laws-inspired-algorithm-cfa.

Keywords: Evolutionary algorithms (EAs) · CFA optimizer · Coulomb's and Franklin's laws · high-dimension group search · global numerical optimization

C. Comito and D. Talia (Eds.): PerSOM 2022, LNICST 494, pp. 111–124, 2023.
https://doi.org/10.1007/978-3-031-31469-8_8

1 Introduction

Recent years have seen the use of Physics-Inspired Algorithms (PIAs), such as Atom Search Optimization (ASO) [1] and Wind Driven Optimization (WDO) [2], to address optimization problems that are challenging in the real world, such as non-linearity, non-smoothness, non-convexity, mixed-integer nature, cubic, and non-differentiability. Two major types of optimization techniques are mathematical computing and evolutionary algorithms. These include quadratic programming, linear programming, direct local search methods [3], Nelder and Mead [4], and trust-region quadratic-based models [5]. However, classical mathematical programming approaches cannot provide practical solutions for various optimization problems due to their complexity.

The second group of proposed techniques are meta-heuristic optimization algorithms, which are inspired and modeled by natural phenomena like collective bird and animal behaviors. Examples include Genetic Algorithm (GA) [6], Parti-cle Swarm Optimization (PSO) [7], Differential Evolution (DE) [8], Honey Bees Optimization (MBO) [9], Bacteria Foraging Optimization (BFO) [10], Harmony Search (HS) [11], Cat Swarm Optimization (CSO) [12], Imperialist Competitive Algorithm (ICA) [13], Artificial Bee Colony (ABC) [14], Biogeography-Based Optimization (BBO) [15], Cuckoo Search (CS) [16], Group Search Optimizer (GSO) [17], Chemical Reaction Optimization (CRO) [18], Teaching–Learning-Based Optimization (TLBO) [19], Grey Wolf Optimizer (GWO) [20], and Ant Colony Optimization (ACO) [21], which were suggested and used to solve global numerical optimization issues. These methods have gained popularity in various fields such as production management, power systems, industrial engineering, engineering design, applied mathematics, etc. due to their ease of use and good performance in providing global optimum or near-optimal solutions.

Optimizing complex control variables with several constraints is common in many real-world applications. With rising dimensions and complexity, the global optimization performance of population-based algorithms in such situations tends to decline [22]. Other related methods can be found in [30–37].

This article introduces and develops the CFA optimizer, which is inspired by Coulomb's and Franklin's laws, for optimal search using electric particle population models. The CFA optimizer is both feasible and efficient in addressing optimization issues. The usefulness and accuracy of the CFA optimizer in discovering global solutions to well-known test functions are evaluated and compared to those of other powerful computational with the goal of clarifying the CFA optimizer's core notable features.

2 CFA Optimizer

Coulomb's and Franklin's laws for collective search based on the CFA optimizer are modelled in this section, and the mathematical model for its parameter adjustment is offered.

2.1 Coulomb's and Franklin's Laws

Electric charges are elementary particles that can be classified as positive or negative, as first introduced by Franklin [23]. Typically, objects have an equal balance of positive and negative charges, but charging an object disrupts this balance. When two charged objects, i and j, are brought close together (with charges qi and qj respectively), they exert an attractive or repulsive force on each other, known as electrostatic force. This force is determined by Coulomb's law, which states that the force between two objects is proportional to the product of their charges and inversely proportional to the square of the distance between them. As it can be seen in Fig. 1, Coulomb's law also includes a vector direction, represented by, that is perpendicular to the line connecting the two objects.

This work was driven by the idea that certain individuals in a population can have a positive or negative impact on the development of others. Using the example of a population of four members, A, B, C, and D, where A is the best and D is the worst, members C and D have a negative influence on B, while member A has a positive influence. The reverse is true for D, where all members except D have a negative influence, and for A, where all members except A have a positive influence. The idea behind this is inspired by Coulomb's law, which states that an individual is attracted to those who have a positive impact on their life and repelled by those who have a negative impact, meaning that the positions of those with a positive impact are added to the individual, while the positions of those with a negative impact are subtracted.

2.2 Maintaining Assumptions Based on Coulomb's Law (Attraction and Repulsion) for Optimization

• First assumption: free and moving point charges

The normal state of objects is characterized by an equal number of positive and negative electrical charges. In this state, objects typically consist of Nob distinct elements, each containing n free and mobile point charges, as is the case in gaseous states. Each point charge, represented by q, is made up of D elementary charges (e) or quantized charges. The ith object (Obi) is assumed to have n point charges, and each point charge is considered a potential solution to a problem, with D representing the number of variables to choose from.

• Second assumption: a sign of point charges

In general, objects are made up of an equal number of positive and negative charges. When considering a population of N distinct objects, each with n free, mobile point charges (such as in the gaseous state), each point charge (q) can be viewed as a potential solution to a problem, with D being the number of decision variables. For a specific point charge (qj) of an object (Obi), other point charges within the same object that have a higher objective function value will repel it. In comparison, those with a lower objective function value will attract it. This concept can be illustrated by considering a population of four individuals, where one individual (A) may be positively influenced by one member (B) and negatively influenced by others (C and D).Third assumption: Probabilistic Ionization.

Ionization is the process of separating an electron from the nucleus due to a lack of electrostatic attraction. The energy required to accomplish this is known as ionization

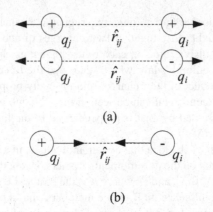

(a)

(b)

Fig. 1. Coulomb's law, a) Electric repulsion force for two charges with the same signs, b) Electric attraction force for two charges with the opposite signs.

energy. In this context, we consider the possibility that the elementary charge of an object, can be replaced with a new elementary charge under the influence of other charges within the same object.

• Fourth assumption: the probabilistic contact of charged objects to each other

v each one exchanges its highest and lowest ranking point charges with the object to its right and receives the highest and lowest ranking point charges from the object to its left. It's important to note that the point charges exchanged may not necessarily become the highest and lowest ranking point charges for the receiving object.

2.3   CFA Optimizer: The Proposed Algorithm

The working procedure of the CFA optimizer is described in this subsection, which is based on motivated mathematical equations of Coulomb's and Franklin's laws. The steps of the CFA optimizer are as follows:

• **Step 1: Initial population**

At the beginning, N initial solutions are randomly generated as a population in the form of N vectors with D dimensions, with each kth element of the vectors within the lower and upper limits of the kth decision variable ($[x_k^{min}, x_k^{max}]$). x_j^i The value of x_j^i is determined within the problem's search area using a uniform random variable $U[0, 1]$ as follows:

$$x_{j,k}^i = x_k^{min} + U[0, 1] \times \left(x_k^{max} - x_k^{min}\right), \text{ for } k = 1, \cdots, D \qquad . \text{ (1)}$$

• **Step 2: Objects selection for** $Nob \geq 2$

When there are multiple objects, the initial population is organized in order of best to worst objective function values and then divided into Nob groups, each group representing a different object. The population is divided by assigning the first member of the arranged population to the first group, the second member to the second group, and so on until all members are assigned to the groups.

- **Step 3: The attraction/repulsion phase**

In this section, we first sort the members or point charges of the ith group or object based on their objective function value. To calculate the new position of the jth member, xj, of the ith group or object, we randomly select alpha/r members with objective function values less or greater than xj for attraction or repulsion, respectively. We then calculate the average of these selected members, which will be used to compute the new position of xj using a mathematical model based on attraction and repulsion. If the objective function value of the new position is better than the old position, it will become the new position of xj, otherwise, xj will retain its previous position.

$$
x_j^{new} = x_j^{old} + \left| \cos \theta_j^{new} \right|^2 \times \left(x^{Best} - x^{Worst} \right) + \left| \sin \theta_j^{new} \right|^2
$$
$$
\times \left(mean \left(\sum_{\substack{m=1 \in \text{Ob}_i}}^{\alpha, \alpha \leq \alpha_{max} \atop \text{Better - than - } x_j} x_m \right) - mean \left(\sum_{\substack{m=1 \in \text{Ob}_i}}^{r, r \leq r_{max} \atop \text{Worse - than - } x_j} x_m \right) \right) \tag{2}
$$

In this section, the process of determining the new position of the jth member (xj) of the ith group (Obi) is described using a mathematical model that takes into account attraction and repulsion forces. First, the members of the ith group are sorted based on the value of their objective function. Then, a random number of members with objective function values that are less or greater than xj are chosen for the attraction and repulsion phases, respectively. The average of these chosen members is calculated and used to update the position of xj using an equation. If the objective function value of the new position is better than the old position, xj's position is updated, otherwise it remains the same. The maximum number of negative and positive charges used in averaging (rmax and rmin) are calculated using equations and are affected by a random variable and initial values that are set to be equal to each other. The effect of this process is demonstrated through an example of charging and discharging based on variations of a certain parameter.

$$
\theta_j^{new} = \theta_j^{old} + U\left(0, \frac{3}{2}\pi\right),
$$
$$
\theta_j^{initial} = U(0, 2\pi). \tag{3}
$$

$$
\alpha_{max} = \alpha_0 * (1 + \cos\theta), \quad r_{max} = r_0 * (1 - \cos\theta), \quad \alpha_0 = r_0. \tag{4}
$$

- **Step 4: Probabilistic ionization phase**

In this phase, the ionization process is performed individually for each member, or point charge, of the group. Only the kth decision variable (xj,k) of the member xj of the population is affected by ionization. If the probability value of the normalized ionization energy Pi for the jth member (xj) is greater than a random value rand, the decision variable xj,k is chosen at random using the equation where D is the number of variables in the optimization problem. The new decision variable is obtained using the kth decision variables of the best member and the worst member of the same group according to Eq. (5).

$$if \ \text{rand}_i \leq Pi \ \text{and} \ k = \text{round}(1 + \text{rand} * (D-1))$$

$$x_{j,k}^{\text{new}} = x_k^{\text{Best}} + x_k^{\text{Worst}} - x_{j,k} \qquad (5)$$

$$x_j = x_j^{\text{new}}$$

• Step 5: Probabilistic contact phase for the multi-object CFA optimizer

The process of contact between groups of charges, or members, is done probabilistically, meaning it is done based on a certain probability. When multiple groups of charges are used, the contact operation is performed if a randomly generated value is greater than a constant value called Pc, which is the contact probability factor. In the case of large-dimensional problems, this value was found to be 0.5, which produced the best results in most simulations. The formula for the probabilistic contact phase is outlined in Eq. 6.

if $\text{rand}_{Iter} \leq Pc$ and $Nob \geq 2$:

$$\begin{cases} x^{\text{Best}_1} = x^{\text{Best}_{Nob}}, \ ..., x^{\text{Best}_{i+1}} = x^{\text{Best}_i}, \ ..., \ x^{\text{Best}_{Nob}} = x^{\text{Best}_{Nob-1}} \\ x^{\text{Worst}_1} = x^{\text{Worst}_{Nob}}, \ ..., x^{\text{Worst}_{i+1}} = x^{\text{Worst}_i}, \ ..., \ x^{\text{Worst}_{Nob}} = x^{\text{Worst}_{Nob-1}} \end{cases} \qquad (6)$$

The flowchart of the optimization process of CFA optimizer is shown in Fig. 2.

Step 1: *Initial population for N charges or N vectors*

$$x_{j,k}^i = x_k^{\min} + U[0,1] \times \left(x_k^{\max} - x_k^{\min} \right), \quad \text{for } k = 1, \cdots, D$$

Step 2: *Objects selection for* $Nob \geq 2$

Produce Nob groups via the initial population

Step 3: *The attraction/repulsion phase*

$$x_j^{\text{new}} = x_j^{\text{old}} + \left| \cos \theta_j^{\text{new}} \right|^2 \times \left(x^{\text{Best}} - x^{\text{Worst}} \right) + \left| \sin \theta_j^{\text{new}} \right|^2$$

$$\times \left(\text{mean} \left(\sum_{m=1 \in \text{Ob}_i}^{\alpha, \alpha \leq \alpha_{\max}} x_m^{\text{Better-than-}x_j} \right) - \text{mean} \left(\sum_{m=1 \in \text{Ob}_i}^{r, r \leq r_{\max}} x_m^{\text{Worse-than-}x_j} \right) \right)$$

if $f\left(x_j^{\text{new}} \right) \leq f\left(x_j^{\text{old}} \right)$

$$x_j = x_j^{\text{new}}$$

end

Step 4: *Probabilistic ionization phase*

if $\text{rand}_i \leq Pi$ and $k = \text{round}\left(1 + \text{rand} * (D-1) \right)$

$$x_{j,k}^{\text{new}} = x_k^{\text{Best}} + x_k^{\text{Worst}} - x_{j,k}$$

end

$$x_j = x_j^{\text{new}}$$

Step 5: *Probabilistic contact phase for multi-object CFA*

if $\text{rand}_{\text{Iter}} \leq Pc$ and $Nob \geq 2$:

$$\begin{cases} x^{\text{Best}_1} = x^{\text{Best}_{Nob}}, \ldots, x^{\text{Best}_{i+1}} = x^{\text{Best}_i}, \ldots, x^{\text{Best}_{Nob}} = x^{\text{Best}_{Nob-1}} \\ x^{\text{Worst}_1} = x^{\text{Worst}_{Nob}}, \ldots, x^{\text{Worst}_{i+1}} = x^{\text{Worst}_i}, \ldots, x^{\text{Worst}_{Nob}} = x^{\text{Worst}_{Nob-1}} \end{cases}$$

end

Fig. 2. Flowchart of the optimization operation of CFA.

3 Experimental Studies

After Sphere (f_1), Rosenbrock (f_2), Rastrigin (f_3), Griewank (f_4), Schwefel-2-21(f_5), Schwefel-1-2 (f_6), and Weierstrass (f_7) [24] are the seven basic test functions that we used to explore and study the performance and robustness of the proposed CFA in different optimization environments. The detailed explanation of the fundamental test functions have been given in Table 1 and in [24].

3.1   Experiment 1: A Competitive Study for Showing CFA Performance

The performance of the CFA optimizer was compared to that of five other advanced optimization algorithms, including hybrid real coded genetic algorithm (RCGA) which combines the global and local search (GL-25) [25] (http://dces.essex.ac.uk/staff/zhang/), DE with strategy adaptation (SaDE) [26] (www.ntu.edu.sg/home/epnsugan), composite DE algorithm (CoDE) [27] (http://dces.essex.ac.uk/staff/zhang/), the improved standard PSO 2011 (SPSO2011) [28] developed by Mahamed G.H. Omran and Maurice Clerc (by Mahamed Omran http://www.particleswarm.info) (SPSO2013) and the heterogeneous comprehensive learning PSO (HCLPSO) with enhanced exploration and exploitation PSO [29] (www.ntu.edu.sg/home/epnsugan) for test on seven basic benchmarks with D = 50. The number of function evaluations (FEs) for all algorithms is FEs = $D * 5000$ and the population size selected for CFA is $N = 20$ and so $Nob = 20/5 = 4$. We employed the identical parameters for these five sophisticated algorithms in this experiment study as the original papers. Thirty separate runs of all algorithms are performed on all of the test functions and issues. This signifies that the performance of each optimization algorithm is either lower than, better than, or similar to that of CFA when compared to the results of CFA and the other five advanced algorithms mentioned as "−", "+", and "=" in the last row of all the best results tables.

Using the identical parameters for all algorithms, the CFA optimizer produced the best results after 30 runs, with the Mean and Standard Deviation (Std.) as listed in Table 2. In this Table, the best findings are given in **boldface**, with the best outcomes for each function. A comparison of the six conventional test functions shows that CFA outperforms the other five algorithms tested. On the test function f_2, the CoDE optimization algorithm outperforms the competition, whereas the SaDE optimization method achieved the same top results with CFA on the test function f_3. CFA outperforms the other five advanced algorithms in this study when it comes to optimizing 50-dimensional test functions.

3.2   Experiment 2: Test on the Effect Pi in the CFA Performance

In this section, we investigate the effectiveness of changing control parameter Pi from 0.01 to 0.9 in CFA optimizer on the four test functions f_1, f_2, f_3, and f_7.

Table 3 displays the computational results the Mean and the Std. For Pi with 0.01, 0.05, 0.25, 0.5, 0.9 values, after 30 runs for the four test functions f_1, f_2, f_3, and f_7, with the conditions as same as the pervious section and Table 2, the best results on each function have been shown in **boldface**. The best results demonstrate that the proposed algorithm shows efficient performance than the other five advanced algorithms for all the different values Pi.

Figure 3 also shows the convergence characteristic of the proposed algorithm with different Pi values to demonstrate the convergence feature. As shown in the bottom image, which is a down-scale version of the top figure, the algorithm converged relatively quickly to the global optimal path, and the varying Pi had no significant effect on its convergence.

The black color is for the Pi of 0.01, the red for 0.05, the pink for 0.1, the blue for 0.25, the green for 0.5 and the yellow for pi equal to 0.9.

f_7: K = 0.01; r = 0.05; m = 0.1, b = 0.25, g = 0.5; y = 0.9.

Table 1. Summary of the selected test functions with fmin = 0.

Test function	Search Range
$f_1 = \sum_{i=1}^{D} x_i^2$	$[-100, 100]D$
$f_2 = \sum_{i=1}^{D-1} (100(x_i^2 - x_{i+1})^2 + (x_i - 1)^2)$	$[-2.048, 2.048]D$
$f_3 = \sum_{i=1}^{D} (x_i^2 - 10\cos(2\pi x_i) + 10)$	$[-5.12, 5.12]D$
$f_4 = \dfrac{1}{4000} \sum_{i=1}^{D} (x_i - 100)^2 - \prod_{i=1}^{D} \cos\left(\dfrac{x_i - 100}{\sqrt{i}}\right) + 1$	$[-600, 600]D$
$f_5(x) = \max_{j=1}^{D} \lvert x_j \rvert$	$[-100, 100]D$
$f_6 = \sum_{i=1}^{D} \left(\sum_{j=1}^{i} x_j\right)^2$	$[-100, 100]D$
$f_7 = \sum_{i=1}^{D} \left(\sum_{k=0}^{k\,\max} \left[a^k \cos\left(2\pi b^k (x_i + 0.5)\right)\right]\right)$ $-D \sum_{k=0}^{k\,\max} \left[a^k \cos\left(2\pi b^k\right)\right],$ $a = 0.5 \ b = 3 \ k\max = 20$	$[-0.50, 0.50]D$

Table 2. Experimental results of all algorithms over 30 independent runs on 7 test functions of 50 variables with 250,000 fes.

F	GL-25	SaDE	CoDE	SPSO2013	HCLPSO	CFA
f_1	5.70E−85	3.67E−44	3.11E−15	9.59E−05	1.84E−18	**0.00E+00**
	3.12E−84	6.35E−44	3.01E−15	4.92E−06	9.78E−09	**0.00E+00**
	−	−	−	−	−	
f_2	4.17E+01	4.41E+01	**3.35E+01**	4.35E+01	4.14E+01	4.36E+01
	8.91E−01	1.56E+00	**5.04E−01**	1.05E+00	3.53E−01	9.66E−01
	−	−	+	−	−	
f_3	5.35E+01	**0.00E+00**	7.64E+01	4.36E+01	7.75E+00	**0.00E+00**
	1.21E+01	**0.00E+00**	6.08E+00	9.34E+00	1.50E+00	**0.00E+00**
	−	=	−	−	−	
f_4	4.18E−03	4.06E−03	5.83E−15	6.60E−03	1.52E−03	**0.00E+00**
	7.24E−03	7.82E−03	7.39E−15	5.72E−03	7.03E−03	**0.00E+00**
	−	−	−	−	−	

(continued)

Table 2. (*continued*)

F	GL-25	SaDE	CoDE	SPSO2013	HCLPSO	CFA
f_5	1.15E+01	3.46E−01	1.95E−03	8.27E+00	5.94E−01	**0.00E+00**
	2.67E+00	6.73E−01	6.11E−04	1.41E+00	8.96E−02	**0.00E+00**
	−	−	-	−	−	
f_6	7.59E+02	2.14E+00	5.76E−01	1.17E−03	2.61E+01	**0.00E+00**
	5.22E+02	1.40E+00	4.16E−01	5.48E−04	1.5E+00	**0.00E+00**
	−	−	−	−	−	
f_7	1.30E+00	1.36E−01	2.11E−04	1.30E+01	8.38E−06	**0.00E+00**
	5.38E−01	1.91E−01	5.62E−05	1.15E+00	4.40E−06	**0.00E+00**
	−	−	L−	−	−	
$-/+/=$	7/0/0	6/0/1	6/1/0	7/0/0	7/0/0	−

Table 3. The computational results for the different values Pi.

Pi	0.01	0.05	0.1	0.25	0.5	0.9
f_1	**0.00E+00**	**0.00E+00**	**0.00E+00**	**0.00E+00**	**0.00E+00**	**0.00E+00**
	0.00E+00	**0.00E+00**	**0.00E+00**	**0.00E+00**	**0.00E+00**	**0.00E+00**
f_2	4.53E+01	4.40E+01	4.42E+01	4.42E+01	4.39E+01	4.40E+01
	2.47E −01	7.33E− 02	1.36E −01	8.20E −02	2.81E −01	2.68E −01
f_3	**0.00E+00**	**0.00E+00**	**0.00E+00**	**0.00E+00**	**0.00E+00**	**0.00E+00**
	0.00E+00	**0.00E+00**	**0.00E+00**	**0.00E+00**	**0.00E+00**	**0.00E+00**
f_7	**0.00E+00**	**0.00E+00**	**0.00E+00**	**0.00E+00**	**0.00E+00**	**0.00E+00**
	0.00E+00	**0.00E+00**	**0.00E+00**	**0.00E+00**	**0.00E+00**	**0.00E+00**

3.3 Experiment 3: Test on the Effect Pc in the CFA Performance

In this section with the conditions as same as the pervious section, we investigate the effectiveness of changing control parameter Pc from 0.01 to 0.9 in the suggested algorithm on the four test functions f_1, f_2, f_3, and f_7.

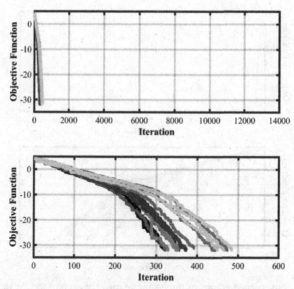

Fig. 3. The convergence graphs of three different runs for each of the Pi values for f_7.

Table 4 show the computational results the Mean and the Std. For Pc with 0.01, 0.05, 0.25, 0.5, 0.9 values, after 30 runs for the four test functions f_1, f_2, f_3, and f_7. The optimal results illustrate that CFA optimizer shows suitable and noticeable performance than the other five advanced algorithms for all the different values Pc.

As in the previous section, to show the CFA convergence characteristic with different Pcs, the convergence characteristic for different values is given in Fig. 4. As can be seen from the figure on the right, which is the down-scale version of the left figure, the CFA quickly converged to the global optimal for this sample test function, and the different Pcs had negligible effect on its convergence.

Table 4. The computational results for the different values Pc.

Pc	0.01	0.05	0.1	0.25	0.5	0.9
f_1	0.00E+00	0.00E+00	0.00E+00	0.00E+00	0.00E+00	0.00E+00
	0.00E+00	0.00E+00	0.00E+00	0.00E+00	0.00E+00	0.00E+00
f_2	4.39E+01	4.40E+01	4.39E+01	4.41E+01	4.42E+01	4.44E+01
	6.03E $-$02	1.95E $-$01	1.69E $-$01	8.32E $-$02	1.57E $-$01	1.74E $-$01
f_3	0.00E+00	0.00E+00	0.00E+00	0.00E+00	0.00E+00	0.00E+00
	0.00E+00	0.00E+00	0.00E+00	0.00E+00	0.00E+00	0.00E+00
f_7	0.00E+00	0.00E+00	0.00E+00	0.00E+00	0.00E+00	0.00E+00
	0.00E+00	0.00E+00	0.00E+00	0.00E+00	0.00E+00	0.00E+00

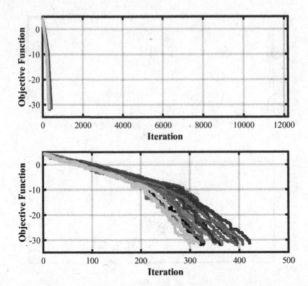

Fig. 4. The convergence graphs of three sample runs for each of the Pc values for f_7.

4 Conclusion

Using a new electrostatics model based on Franklin's and Coulomb's laws called CFA, this research investigates how well the CFA optimizer, a novel and notable technique, performs when used to optimize numerical problems using seven well-known fundamental functions. Population-based algorithms like the CFA optimizer can be used to a wide variety of populations, including groups, individuals, and electric particles. The optimization of CFA includes the stages of attraction and repulsion, probabilistic ionization, and probabilistic contact phases. It was shown that CFA was able to outperform five advanced algorithms, i.e. GL-25, SaDE, CoDE, SPSO2011, and HCLPSO, for solving the benchmark functions. Based on our tests, we can conclude that the CFA optimizer we have proposed outperforms the majority of other test functions for high-dimension optimization tasks despite its simple design and straightforward implementation.

References

1. Zhao, W., Wang, L., Zhang, Z.: Atom search optimization and its application to solve a hydrogeologic parameter estimation problem. Knowl. Based Syst **163**, 283–304 (2019)
2. Bayraktar, Z., Komurcu, M., Werner, D.H.: Wind driven optimization (WDO): a novel nature-inspired optimization algorithm and its application to electromagnetics. In: 2010 IEEE Antennas and Propagation Society International Symposium, p. 1–4. (2010)
3. Hooke, R., Jeeves, T.A.: Direct search solution of numerical and statistical problems. J ACM **8**, 212–229 (1961)
4. Nelder, J.A., Mead, R.: A simplex method for function minimization. Comput J **7**, 308–313 (1965)
5. Winfield, D.H.: Function and functional optimization by interpolation in data tables. Harvard University (1970)

6. Mitchell, M.: An Introduction to Genetic Algorithms. MIT press, Cambridge (1998)
7. Eberhart, R., Kennedy, J.: A new optimizer using particle swarm theory. In: In MHS'95. Proceedings of the Sixth International Symposium on Micro Machine and Human Science, pp. 39-43 (1995)
8. Storn, R., Price, K.: Differential evolution–a simple and efficient heuristic for global optimization over continuous spaces. J Glob Optim 11, 341–359 (1997)
9. Abbass, H.A.: MBO: Marriage in honey bees optimization-A haplometrosis polygynous swarming approach. In: Proceedings of the 2001 Congress Evolutionary Computation (IEEE Cat. No. 01TH8546), vol. 1, p. 207–14 (2001)
10. Passino, K.M.: Biomimicry of bacterial foraging for distributed optimization and control. IEEE Control Syst Mag 22, 52–67 (2002)
11. Lee, K.S., Geem, Z.W.: A new meta-heuristic algorithm for continuous engineering optimization: harmony search theory and practice. Comput. Methods Appl. Mech. Eng. 194, 3902–3933 (2005)
12. Chu, S.-C., Tsai, P.-W., Pan, J.-S.: Cat swarm optimization. In: Yang, Q., Webb, G. (eds.) PRICAI 2006. LNCS (LNAI), vol. 4099, pp. 854–858. Springer, Heidelberg (2006). https://doi.org/10.1007/978-3-540-36668-3_94
13. Atashpaz-Gargari, E., Lucas, C.: Imperialist competitive algorithm: an algorithm for optimization inspired by imperialistic competition. In: 2007 IEEE Congress on Evolutionary Computation, p. 4661–7 (2007)
14. Karaboga, D., Basturk, B.: A powerful and efficient algorithm for numerical function optimization: artificial bee colony (ABC) algorithm. J Glob Optim 39, 459–471 (2007)
15. Simon, D.: Biogeography-based optimization. IEEE Trans Evol Comput 12, 702–713 (2008)
16. Yang, X-S., Deb, S.: Cuckoo search via Lévy flights. 2009 World Congr. Nat Biol inspired Comput, p. 210–214 (2009)
17. He, S., Wu, Q.H., Saunders, J.R.: Group search optimizer: an optimization algorithm inspired by animal searching behavior. IEEE Trans. Evol. Comput. 13, 973–990 (2009)
18. Lam, A.Y.S., Li, V.O.K.: Chemical-reaction-inspired metaheuristic for optimization. IEEE Trans. Evol. Comput. 14, 381–399 (2009)
19. Rao, R.V., Savsani, V.J., Vakharia, D.P.: Teaching–learning-based optimization: an optimization method for continuous non-linear large scale problems. Inf. Sci. 183, 1–15 (2012)
20. Mirjalili, S., Mirjalili, S.M., Lewis, A.: Grey wolf optimizer. Adv. Eng. Softw. 69, 46–61 (2014)
21. Drigo, M.: The ant system: optimization by a colony of cooperating agents. IEEE Trans. Syst. Man, Cybern. B 26, 1–13 (1996)
22. Mahdavi, S., Shiri, M.E., Rahnamayan, S.: Metaheuristics in large-scale global continues optimization: a survey. Inf. Sci. 295, 407–428 (2015)
23. Halliday D, Resnick R, Walker J. Fundamentals of physics. John Wiley \& Sons; 2013
24. Li, C., Yang, S., Nguyen, T.T.: A self-learning particle swarm optimizer for global optimization problems. IEEE Trans. Syst. Man, Cybern. Part B 42, 627–646 (2011)
25. García-Martínez, C., Lozano, M., Herrera, F., Molina, D., Sánchez, A.M.: Global and local real-coded genetic algorithms based on parent-centric crossover operators. Eur. J. Oper. Res. 185, 1088–1113 (2008)
26. Qin, A.K., Huang, V.L., Suganthan, P.N.: Differential evolution algorithm with strategy adaptation for global numerical optimization. IEEE Trans. Evol. Comput. 13, 398–417 (2008)
27. Wang, Y., Cai, Z., Zhang, Q.: Differential evolution with composite trial vector generation strategies and control parameters. IEEE Trans. Evol. Comput. 15, 55–66 (2011)
28. Zambrano-Bigiarini, M., Clerc, M., Rojas, R.: Standard particle swarm optimisation 2011 at cec-2013: A baseline for future pso improvements. In: 2013 IEEE Congress Evolutionary Computation, p. 2337–2344 (2013)

29. Lynn, N., Suganthan, P.N.: Heterogeneous comprehensive learning particle swarm optimization with enhanced exploration and exploitation. Swarm Evol. Comput. **24**, 11–24 (2015)

30. Gul, F., et al.: A Centralized Strategy for Multi-Agent Exploration. IEEE Access **10**, 126871–126884 (2022)

31. Abualigah, L., Elaziz, M.A., Khodadadi, N., Forestiero, A., Jia, H., Gandomi, A.H.: Aquila optimizer based PSO swarm intelligence for IoT task scheduling application in cloud computing. In: Houssein, E.H., Abd Elaziz, M., Oliva, D., Abualigah, L. (Eds.) Integrating Meta-Heuristics and Machine Learning for Real-World Optimization Problems. Studies in Computational Intelligence, vol. 1038, pp. 481–497. Springer, Cham. (2022). https://doi.org/10.1007/978-3-030-99079-4_19

32. Abualigah, L., Forestiero, A., Elaziz, M.A.: Bio-inspired agents for a distributed NLP-based clustering in smart environments. In: Abraham, A., et al. (eds.) SoCPaR 2021. LNNS, vol. 417, pp. 678–687. Springer, Cham (2022). https://doi.org/10.1007/978-3-030-96302-6_64

33. Alzu'bi, D., et al.: Kidney tumor detection and classification based on deep learning approaches: a new dataset in CT scans. J. Healthc. Eng. 2022 (2022)

34. Khazalah, A., et al.: Image processing identification for sapodilla using convolution neural network (CNN) and transfer learning techniques. In: Abualigah, L. (Eds.) Classification Applications with Deep Learning and Machine Learning Technologies. Studies in Computational Intelligence, vol. 1071, pp. 107–127. Springer, Cham (2023). https://doi.org/10.1007/978-3-031-17576-3_5

35. Melhem, M.K.B., Abualigah, L., Zitar, R.A., Hussien, A.G., Oliva, D.: Comparative study on Arabic text classification: challenges and opportunities. In: Abualigah, L. (eds.) Classification Applications with Deep Learning and Machine Learning Technologies. Studies in Computational Intelligence, vol. 1071, pp. 217–224. Springer, Cham (2023). https://doi.org/10.1007/978-3-031-17576-3_10

36. Anuar, N.A. et al.: Rambutan image classification using various deep learning approaches. In: Abualigah, L. (eds.) Classification Applications with Deep Learning and Machine Learning Technologies. Studies in Computational Intelligence, vol. 1071, pp. 23–43. Springer, Cham (2023). https://doi.org/10.1007/978-3-031-17576-3_2

37. Ke, C. et al.: Mango varieties classification-based optimization with transfer learning and deep learning approaches. In: Abualigah, L. (ed.) Classification Applications with Deep Learning and Machine Learning Technologies. Studies in Computational Intelligence, vol. 1071, pp. 45–65. Springer, Cham (2023). https://doi.org/10.1007/978-3-031-17576-3_3

A Review of Space Exploration and Trajectory Optimization Techniques for Autonomous Systems: Comprehensive Analysis and Future Directions

Faiza Gul[1]([✉]), Imran Mir[2], Uzma Gul[3], and Agostino Forestiero[4]([✉])

[1] Aerospace and Aviation Campus Kamra, Air University, Kamra, Pakistan
gulfaiza@outlook.com, faiza.gul@aack.au.edu.pk
[2] School of Avionics and Electrical Engineering, College of Aeronautical Engineering, NUST, Risalpur, Pakistan
imir@cae.nust.edu.pk
[3] Department of Telecommunication, University of Engineering and Technology (UET), Taxila, Pakistan
[4] Institute for High-Performance Computing and Networking National Research Council of Italy, Rome, Italy
agostino.forestiero@icar.cnr.it

Abstract. Autonomous systems have achieved great success over the last couple of decades. They have bring the revolutionary change in the world, either its ground vehicles, aerial systems or underground vehicles. Number of research papers have been written on the importance of autonomous systems and their applications in different field. Keeping in view the pattern of research done by authors, an effort has been made to provide a single platform for readers to familiarize themselves with applications involved in terrestrial, aerial and undersea systems along with different sets of dimensions involved in achieving these applications. Therefore, the article provides a summary of the main communication methods used by terrestrial, aerial, and undersea space research vehicles. In addition to providing an exhaustive summary of the difficulties encountered in trajectory planning, space exploration, optimization, and other areas, the research also presents optimization methods applicable to aerial, undersea, and terrestrial applications. As the literature lacks extensive studies like this one, hence an effort has been made to fill the gap for readers interested in path design. This study tackles numerical, bioinspired, and hybrid techniques for each of the dimensions given. With this study, we attempted to provide a single repository for a plethora of research on autonomous land vehicles, their trajectory optimization, as well as research on aerial and undersea vehicles. The article ends with the most practical directions for future research.

Keyword: Space exploration · Undersea Vehicle · Aerial Vehicle · Terrestrial Vehicle

C. Comito and D. Talia (Eds.): PerSOM 2022, LNICST 494, pp. 125–138, 2023.
https://doi.org/10.1007/978-3-031-31469-8_9

1 Introduction

The significance of driver-less vehicles was initiated dated back in 2007 by DARPA (Defense Advanced Research Projects Agency) Urban challenge [9], the concept was later on extended for the development of underwater and aerial vehicles. In order to increase the flying stability of the aerial system, many concepts were applied to flight dynamics methods [29]. The concept further exploited in numerous ways, which result in development of number of algorithms and opened new areas for research. Since the 1970s, route planning has attracted a lot of interest. It has been applied to a variety of issues, from basic geographic route planning to selecting the best course of action to achieve a specific objective. Path planning uses input from system-mounted sensors to update environmental maps and direct the motions of the robot or planned autonomous vehicle (AV) in environments that are wholly unknown, partially unknown, or both. For both ground and airborne vehicles, numerous techniques have been developed during the past ten years using the trajectory optimization issue. The two categories of these trajectory optimization issues are a) heuristics and b) non-heuristic approaches. In order to produce optimal solutions, the former uses trade-offs, which produce findings that are computationally efficient, whilst the latter requires mathematical derivations, which are computationally expensive. The optimization algorithms used in applications of ground robotics [17] includes numerous applications. Autonomous navigation is an essential component of moving robots or aerial vehicles. It helps them depend less on support from people. It does, however, involve a number of tasks or challenges to overcome, such path planning. Choosing the most effective plan to get a robot from its current state to the desired state is the aim of this assignment. For instance, the objective and the starting point could both be the same condition. This action plan known as a path or route. The robot is guided to the desired location using the path. Path planning algorithms often seek out the ideal path, or a close approximation of it. The optimal route is the best path in the sense that it is the outcome of decreasing one or more objective optimization functions. For instance, this route can be the one that travels the quickest. This is essential in missions like search-and-rescue efforts, as disaster victims may ask for help in life-or-death situations [21]. The robot's energy consumption may be another optimization factor to take into account. This is crucial in the case of planetary exploration because rovers only have a finite amount of energetic resources at their disposal. The purpose of the suggested survey article on these vehicles navigation is to discover the research gaps and potential for innovation in a certain field. The route generation and optimization problem can be tackled using deterministic (numerical) approaches, nature-inspired algorithms, or a combination of these techniques. For calculating the precise solution, there are several deterministic techniques available, including the Iterative method [24], Runge Kutta [14], Newton Raphson method [34], and Bisection method [35]. These algorithms are used to tackle path planning, trajectory optimization, and a variety of other vehicle versions for autonomous vehicles. Swarm based approaches are dependent on the social hierarchy of animals and birds such as ants, bees, and flies. There are great number of different algorithms which are inspired from the nature such as Grey Wolf Optimizer, Whale Optimization, Deer Hunting Algorithm, Slap Swarm

Algorithm, Grasshopper Algorithm, Ant Lion Optimizer, Moth Flame Optimizer, Simulated Annealing, Arithmetic Algorithm, Harmony Search Algorithm, Aquila Optimizer, and Owl Search Algorithm [9] (Fig. 1).

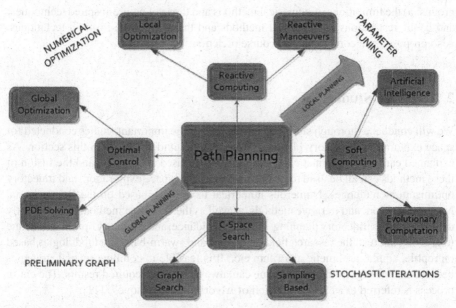

Fig. 1. Schematic showing different Path Planning Methods. (Mir, I., Gul, F., Mir, S., Khan, M.A., Saeed, N., Abualigah, L., Abuhaija, B., Gandomi, A.H.: A survey of trajectory planning techniques for autonomous systems. Electronics **11**(18), 2801 (2022))

1.1 Objective and Contents

The proposed survey paper looks at numerical approaches and nature-inspired strategies for navigation, space exploration and obstacle avoidance used in the literature for land, airborne, and underwater vehicles, as well as how they might be combined or used separately. The goal of the study is to give academics the most recent information required for path optimization, space exploration and environment modeling. The goal of the study is to compare several algorithms and demonstrate how they might be used in different situations. The contributions made by this review are listed below: -

Consolidation of Relevant Work: Amazingly, human being are able to detect their surroundings, maintain control, and make the necessary motor movements all at once. Researchers from all over the world are working on developing intelligent autonomous vehicle which can independently take decisions while exploring the environment. The vehicle may also possess attributes like human beings, and can maneuver while maintaining safety and ensuring that the vehicle's efficiency is not compromised. In order for readers to comprehend the value of land, airborne, and underwater vehicles in industrial research, this essay aims to offer them significant insight.

Limitations with Future Direction: This research's significant additional contribution is its use of numerical and nature-inspired techniques to pinpoint the difficulties in path optimization and obstacle avoidance. The traits that do not help with determining the best trajectory optimization for both ground and aerial vehicles are identified and divided into groups: a) the limitations of numerical methods and those of nature-inspired techniques; and b) the restrictions of numerical methods and those of nature-inspired techniques. Also proposed is a comprehensive course of action.

2 Relevant Studies

We will conduct a thorough study and assessment of the important studies conducted for space exploration, trajectory planning for automatic guided vehicle in this section. As explained earlier, deterministic techniques, swarm-based algorithms, and the fusion of these methods can all be used to handle path planning, space exploration, and trajectory optimization challenges. Numerous numerical techniques based on the Runge Kutta, Newton Raphson, and Iterative methods, as well as the Bisection method, are frequently used. To address trajectory planning, obstacle avoidance, and trajectory optimization, due to growing interest, the research field broadened and swarm-based methodologies based on reptile, aquila, arithmetic algorithm etc.. It is feasible to combine several strategies because no one algorithm or technique can always give the required results. The entire process is referred to as "Hybridization of Algorithms/Techniques" [11].

2.1 Deterministic Techniques Framework

Deterministic analysis includes the application of algorithms to get numerical solutions. It requires theoretical mathematical study. This section introduces the numerical approaches and their utility in all automatic guided vehicles.

Applications to Aerial Vehicles. The performance of the sensors is the key component of any aerial vehicle system. The effectiveness and dynamics of aerial vehicles are influenced by a variety of sensors, including radars, lidars, and sonars. Owen et al. [25] successfully used radar to find moving targets, while [22] used LiDars for airborne use. There are number of areas which can be studied in aerial vehicle. When a collision happens, Mansury et al. developed a penalty function in a planned path [20]. One technique penalizes the goal function when the planned path gets close to an obstruction, whereas the other penalizes the objective function only when the planned path would cause a collision. In place of a single point, obstacles can alternatively be handled as flight-restricted zones. By using a collocation strategy, Zhao et al. [40] used the nonlinear programming solver to numerically resolve the parameter optimization portion of the optimum control problem (NPSOL) [7]. The results of the NPSOL programme show that after a successful convergence, the non-linear programming problem has a locally optimal solution. Z. Czyz et al. [5] the study looks at aluminium beams joined by flat bars and angle irons as a thin-walled support platform for an unmanned aerial vehicle. The building serves as a form of frame for the propulsion system of the created aircraft, a hybrid multicopter-gyrocopter. To explore the stresses and strains that are associated to this construction's profiles, it was tested under a variety of load patterns. The finite element technique (FEM) and Solid-Works software were used to do the numerical computations, and the load patterns are related to different propeller operating condition. The support platform's separate components' ability to operate in an elastic manner was the subject of the research.

Applications to Ground Vehicles. Online route planning frequently uses curve interpolation planners like Clothoid, Polynomial, Spline, and Bezier curves. These planners have a minimal computing cost since the behaviour of the curve is controlled by a limited set of control parameters, comparable to graph search approaches. The final route's optimization cannot be guaranteed because the dynamic restrictions of a robot have not been considered during the planning stage, necessitating the smoothing step. The measure for uncontrollable divergence is cited by Zhang et al. [37]. Using this statistic, a system is developed to switch between various predictive controllers quickly while preserving predictive accuracy. The computer-based dynamical analysis of engineering systems requires robust and effective numerical methods as a prerequisite. For the analysis, simulation, and optimization of the complex dynamical behaviour of vehicles and vehicle components, as well as their interactions with hydraulics, electronics, and control systems, multibody system dynamics methodologies and software tools provide the integration platform. The modelling of vehicles and their parts, which is based on the principles of classical mechanics, yields nonlinear systems of ordinary differential equations (ODEs) or differential algebraic equations (DAEs) of moderate dimension, which describe the dynamical behaviour in the required frequency range and with a level of detail that is characteristic of vehicle system dynamics. The majority of real-world issues in this area can be reduced to standard numerical mathematics issues, such as explicit ODEs or DAEs with a typical semi-explicit structure in dynamical analysis and systems of nonlinear equations in (quasi-)static analysis. The use of sophisticated, publicly accessible numerical software that is based on widely accepted numerical techniques, such as the Newton-Raphson iteration for nonlinear equations or Runge-Kutta and linear multistep methods for ODE/DAE time integration, is made possible by this transformation to mathematical standard problems. Utilizing a particular structure of the mathematical models for vehicle system dynamics, significant speedups of these numerical standard approaches may be accomplished [3]. The Clothoid curve offers a cutting-edge method for shortening routes and changing curvature. This method, which takes into account two points on the plane, yields a solution to join 2-Clothoid sets in-order to determine the location of a waypoint. The technique aids the robot in fast maneuvering, and motion performance is enhanced [16].

Application to Undersea Vehicles. In terms of relevance, autonomous undersea vehicle systems (AUVs) navigation and controls are now on par with those of terrestrial and aerial vehicles. An alternative name for them is ocean vehicle navigation. Path planning is necessary for autonomous underwater vehicles (AUVs), just like it is for ground and aerial vehicles, in order to navigate as efficiently. The water environment, in contrast to ground and airborne vehicles, presents a number of challenges due to limitations in data transmission, sensing range, and power.

Underwater communication is challenging due of the bandwidth channel's erratic changing. Therefore, choosing the best course of action for autonomous underwater vehicles is a challenging task. Using the Normalized Generalized Velocity Components (NGVC) as a tool for analysis, the author [12] proposed a novel technique that entails two steps: (i) the development of a velocity control algorithm, and (ii) its application to the vehicle dynamics investigation. The decomposition of the inertia matrix leads to altered equations of motion, which are used to define the algorithm. Before carrying out an actual experiment, the author suggested that the approach be used to perform numerical testing of the assumed model for fully functional underwater vehicles. The effectiveness of the suggested method is demonstrated through simulation on a 6 DOF underwater vehicle. In [30], a nonlinear MPC is suggested for an autonomous underwater vehicle (AUV). To solve the path planning problem, a receding horizon optimization framework with a Spline template is employed. Combining the path planning outcome and MPC is used for tracking control.

2.2 Swarm-Based Framework

Without the aid of a third party coordinator, swarm intelligence systems are capable of acting in unison. Swarm intelligence adds a new characteristic to artificial intelligence that allows for the study of emergent features and collective behavior of complex systems in predetermined environments. Many scholars have taken on the problem of planning the trajectory of terrestrial and aerial vehicles using an optimization method that imitates the behavior of living creatures [39]. The issue of trajectory tracking is a very active academic topic. Numerous established techniques, including Artificial Potential Field, Neural Network, Distance Wave Transform, A-star algorithm, and D-star algorithm, are used to solve this problem. These algorithms, also referred to as swarm-based approaches, and have been applied in engineering to tackle difficult mathematical problems.

The correct assessment of the landing place in the shortest possible time is made possible by the incorporation of bio-inspiring algorithms in UAV control systems. The Bats Optimization Algorithm, Moth Flame Optimization Algorithm, and Artificial Bee Colony Algorithm are bio-inspired optimization algorithms used in by Ilango et al. [15] to determine the coordinates (points) of the computed path and to determine the best point of landing, ensuring that the aforementioned parameters are within the operational limits of the UAV. The goal of the research project was to quickly locate the best landing point from the computed points and to establish the path from those points. The error rate is defined as the difference between the initial points of the real path and the derived computed points of the estimated path. The accuracy in forecasting the landing site and the computation time are two trade-off factors used to evaluate the performance of the algorithms.

Application to Aerial Vehicles. The notion of intelligent micro drones that are inspired by soaring insects like bees is presented in [4]. The demonstrated micro drones can carry out sophisticated tasks on their own utilizing basic sensors and very little processing power. In particular, we offer a set of algorithms for navigating, flying in swarm formation, avoiding obstacles, and mapping that are all based on sub-gram sensors and suitable for micro drones' on-board computing. We draw the conclusion that many bio-inspired problems can be completed without the usage of high resolution visual sensors using both simulation and field testing. Autonomous micro drones can also participate in a variety of research domains, such as swarm algorithms for search and rescue and mobile sensor networks. The significance of bio-inspired algorithms (BIAs) is growing dramatically as a result of their potential to optimize numerous issues in a variety of domains, including artificial intelligence, medicine, and other professions. Unmanned aerial vehicles (UAVs) are currently using BIAs because of their autonomy in applications like the internet of things (IoT), autonomous area searching and reconnaissance, etc. Usman et al. [33], uses the particle swarm optimization (PSO) algorithm and a few characteristics of the penguin search optimization algorithm were combined to present an UAV reconnaissance strategy. The main goal of the strategy was to use UAVs to locate the rescue targets by maximizing their movement using combined PSO and PeSOA attributes. Analysis of the results is done using PeSOA attributes both with and without grouping scenarios. Majd Saied et al. [27] examined several UAV. The proposed idea calculates velocity using the ABC approach in order to avoid obstacles and keep track of flight data. In MATLAB, numerous case studies were used to execute the simulations.

Application to Terrestrial Vehicles. A form of intelligent computing technology known as a"bioinspired intelligent algorithm" (BIA) has a more realistic biological functioning mechanism than other varieties. BIAs have advanced significantly in their comprehension of biological and neurological systems as well as in its application to a variety of fields. One of the primary applications of BIAs that has gained increasing attention is mobile robot control. This is because mobile robots can be used widely and because general artificial intelligent algorithms encounter a development roadblock in this area due to complex computing and the reliance on high-precision sensors. In order to aid in a thorough and precise knowledge of BIAs, the author Jianjun et al. [23] provides a summary of recent research in BIAs. The research is concentrated on the realization of various BIAs based on various working mechanisms and the applications for mobile robot control. The survey is divided into four main sections: a classification of BIAs from the perspective of the biomimetic mechanism, an overview of several typical BIAs from various levels, a look at the current uses of BIAs in mobile robot control, and a discussion of some potential future research directions.

Application to Undersea Vehicles. Sanchez et al. [28] suggest a restoration technique whose cost function (objective function) is a No-Reference Image Quality measure and estimates the model parameters using bio-inspired optimization metaheuristics (NR-IQA). The Artificial Bee-Colony Algorithm (ABC), Opposition-based Artificial Bee Colony (OABC), Differential Evolution (DE) metaheuristics, Opposition-based Particle Swarm Optimization (OPSO), Repulsive-Attractive Particle Swarm Optimization (RAPSO), and Artificial Bee Colony Algorithm (ABC) have all been put to the test in this case. P^etr'es et al. [41] a fresh technique based on quick marching that extracts a continuous path from the surroundings while accounting for underwater currents. The path planning problem was put forth as an optimization framework by Yilmaz et al. [36], who combined it with an approach based on integer linear programming. The above-mentioned methods were all tested in two-dimensional (2D) environments, which does not satisfy the actual needs of AUV route planning. Hu et al. [13] researchers created a vision-based autonomous robotic fish with 3D mobility by employing a control rule with an attracting force toward a target and a repulsive force against obstacles.

2.3 Hybrid Techniques Framework

This section provides thorough information on hybridized algorithms and its related to terrestrial, aerial, and undersea applications after elaborating on deterministic and swarm-based methodologies.

Application to Aerial Vehicles. In order to create an ideal path, Xiangyin et al. [38] research provides an upgraded fireworks algorithm (FWA) and particle swarm optimization (PSO) cooperation method. This paper treats the unmanned aerial vehicle (UAV) global path planning as an optimization problem with many constraints. The UAV flight route goal function is modelled to have the shortest length while adhering to stringent multiple threat area constraints. One of the essential presumptions for successful (UWSN) operations is the timely and safe passage of the UAV. Finding a good path in an area with many obstacles and making sure the path can effectively get to the goal location are both important and difficult tasks. In order to ensure that UAVs collect data efficiently in emergency situations, the authors in [26] suggests the hybrid path planning (HPP) algorithm. The probabilistic roadmap (PRM) algorithm and the optimised artificial bee colony (ABC) algorithm are used in the proposed HPP scheme to design the shortest trajectory map and improve various path constraints in a three-dimensional environment, respectively. UAVs offer a platform for carrying out a wide range of jobs, but path planning is essential to every single one of them. It assists in creating a path that is clear of impediments, has a short length, uses less fuel, travels faster, and steers the aircraft and its associated antenna power signature safely around the hostile antenna to avoid detection. B. Abhishek et al. [1] study introduces two novel hybrid algorithms, particle swarm optimization (PSO) with harmony search algorithm and PSO with genetic algorithm, to enhance path planning to take into account all the aforementioned restrictions. In contrast to the current algorithms, which are inclined towards either an exploitative search or an exploratory search, the hybrid algorithms execute both an exploratory and an exploitative search.

Application to Terrestrial Vehicles. Shang Erke et al. [6] introduces different setps, firstly a standard for evaluating algorithms is presented, allowing for the performance of various algorithms to be measured and suitable parameters to be chosen for the proposed method. Second, a global planning or human-generated guideline is used to construct a heuristic function to address the drawback of conventional A-Star algorithms. Thirdly, key points around the obstacle are used to improve obstacle avoidance performance. These points would direct the planning path to avoid the obstacle much earlier than the conventional one. Fourth, to shorten the suggested algorithm's computation time, a novel variable-step based A-Star algorithm is also introduced. Experimental results demonstrate that the performance of the proposed algorithm is robust and stable when compared to state-of-the-art methods.

Rafal et al. [31] Robotic palletizing is a typical use of industrial robotization. The robotic arm may frequently manage more than one production line due to its efficiency. In this situation, choosing the right product from one of numerous production lines will have an impact on total efficiency. In this work, a single robotic arm controlling three production lines is taken into consideration. Each item's cycle time and maximum permitted waiting time are taken into consideration. Constrained multi-objective optimization issues were created as a result of the authors' four separate objective functions they provided in relation to potential requirements in a factory environment. The Artificial Bee Colony algorithm, which is backed by Deb's rules, has been used to tackle this issue. Results have been compared using three fundamental decision-making processes and the Reinforcement Learning methodology. It has been demonstrated that the suggested approach both greatly boosts production rate and satisfies specific requirements, such as minimum energy consumption per palletized item ratio and equal container filling.

Rafal et al. [32] introduces a novel technique for local minimum avoidance. It is based on the establishment of imaginary barriers known as top quarks in crucial locations. The APF-based path planner is further repelled by these barriers. The new temporary objective for APF was chosen with consideration for the projected AGV trajectory that was free of stagnation. Combining these techniques enables one to shorten the distance travelled, enhance its smoothness, and avoid local minima. The Husarion ROSbot 2.0 PRO mobile robot was used to test the suggested Predictive Artificial Potential Field (PAPF) algorithm, and the findings, which are presented as movies, are also included as supplemental files. The proposed path planning algorithm enables a 21.4% reduction in the amount of electricity used when compared to the original APF. Up to 8.73% shorter paths and up to 40.23% faster times to the goal position were made possible by PAPF. When using the proposed algorithm, the AGV moves significantly more smoothly, and the proposed top-quarks-based local minimum avoidance mechanism enables bypassing of the local minima.

Undersea Vehicles. The path planning scenario for an autonomous underwater vehicle (AUV) is presented by Hui et al. [19] as an optimization problem constrained by a mix of hard and soft constraints. The goal of the path planner is to create the best path in both 2D and 3D for navigating an AUV safely through an ocean environment with known obstructions and irregular currents. The path planner employs the selectively Differential Evolution (DE)-hybridized Quantum PSO (SDEQPSO) and Adaptive PSO particle swarm optimization (PSO) algorithms (SDEAPSO). In a series of thorough Monte Carlo simulations and ANOVA (analysis of variance) methods, the performances of the path planners under various restrictions are examined based on their individual solution characteristics, stabilities, and computing effectiveness. Based on the simulation results, it was discovered that the SDEQPSO path planner, which uses a hard constraint for the boundary condition and a soft constraint for obstacle avoidance, is more effective than other algorithms at generating feasible and smooth AUV paths. This is demonstrated by its relatively low computational requirement and excellent solution quality.

Hui et al. [18] the paper describes the use of an open-source system architecture called MOOS-IvP to construct an online path planner in an autonomous underwater vehicle (AUV) system. The path planner used the selective differential evolution quantum-behaved particle swarm optimization (SDEQPSO) algorithm together with a path replanning scheme. The solution was built on a modular structure to guarantee the path replanner's reliability throughout a mission. In hardware-in-the-loop (HIL) experiments, the path replanner interacted with the onboard controllers and actuators of an Explorer AUV to assess and verify its performance under stochastic processes. The experimental findings shown that the path replanner may be used in real time to design and continually improve a safe and practicable path for a dynamic and uncharted environment using technology onboard an Explorer AUV.

3   Challenges, Recommendation and Future Directions

Based on a review of the literature, we provide a quick overview of the difficulties faced during the space exploration process in this section. Then, we'll suggest some fixes and potential future directions.

3.1   Challenges

Despite the fact that there are number of research contributions for land, aerial and underwater vehicles but it is observed that no single method guarantees 100% results. The fundamental disadvantage of all swarm-based algorithms is their inherent tendency to become trapped in local or global maxima or minima. Similar to oscillations, undesired noise, and overshooting, controllers make faults in output. These drawbacks have a significant effect on how an algorithm functions, which in turn affects how well autonomous vehicles operate. Another challenge is that various algorithms rely their navigational predictions on environmental data. Unwanted halt in the vehicle's motion result from this.

3.2   Proposed Solutions

Path planning, which is now further expanded to path optimization, is one of the most researched issues in control engineering for terrestrial, aerial, and undersea vehicles. In order to tackle optimization issues in all three domains, several algorithms using probabilistic and non-probabilistic methods have been used, including A-star, bug, bug2, evolutionary algorithm, probabilistic roadmap, rolling window algorithms, etc. These techniques have variety of versions, including Astar and D-star as well as numerous enhancements to PRM and APF algorithms are available. No method is capable of achieving all objectives, hence method integration and hybridization have become widespread practices. The social behaviours of numerous creatures were imitated in the form of swarm-based algorithms, then they are modelled as full optimization algorithms. Nature-inspired algorithms are frequently employed in this context, including the Aquila Optimizer, Arithmetic Optimizer, Snake Optimizer, and Reptile search Optimizer. Researchers are also combining methods inspired by nature to create controllers with names like sliding mode controller, adaptive controller, and linear quadratic controller. The best strategy is to combine several approaches, keeping in mind the trends involved in the execution of various algorithms, so that numerous objectives can be reached rather than just one [10]. The disadvantage of hybridization is that, it may lead to more noise, increase oscillations in system performance, or more complex computations. Even yet, the additional benefits following integration are incomparable to other shortcomings. Under such circumstances, trade-offs are always there.

3.3 Potential Future Directions

In order to give an insight for the reader to study potential topics for trajectory generation, utilizing the recently created Reptile Search Optimizer, which has widespread potential use, is one possible direction to work in. The Reptile Search optimizer (RSA) is an algorithm with natural design cues [2]. This slightly modified, swarm-based reptile search optimizer combined with a multi-coordinated agent exploring. These techniques for area surfing and trajectory optimization may be of interest to readers. A similar has been implemented and can be found in [8].

Table 1. Benefits and Weakness Involved in Autonomous Vehicles

Algorithms	Benefits	Weakness	Implementation
Fuzzy Logic	(a) Easy tunning of fuzzy rules (b) Easy to learn (c) Integration with other algorithms are easy	(a) Membership functions cannot be easily implemented	Simulated world and Real time
Neural Network	(a) Easy implementation as compared to fuzzy rules (b) Logic building is easy (c) Back-propagation is found beneficial	(a) Understanding of Neuron layers are hard (b) Multiple Layered structure aids in the complexity	Real time and simulation
Genetic Algorithm	(a) Convergence rate is fast (b) Easily to integrate	(a) Local/global minima/maxima problem exists in complex environment (b) Fine tuning is required	Simulated world
ABC	(a) Control variables are less (b) Lesser execution time is needed (c) Integrate-able with other algorithms	(a) Convergence rate is slow	Simulated world

(continued)

Table 1. (*continued*)

Algorithms	Benefits	Weakness	Implementation
Arithmetic Algorithm	(a) Easy Implementation	(a) Convergence rate is slow	Simulated world
GWO	(a) Convergence rate is fast (b) Tuning of parameter is easy (c) When integrated with other algorithm performs better	(a) Bit tricky in complex environment	Simulated world
Moth flame	(a) Perform better in complex environment	(a) Suffers from premature convergence	Simulated world and Real time
WOA	(a) Convergence rate is fast	(a) Implementation in dynamic environment is hard	Simulated world and Real time
Aquila Optimizer	(a) Effective in producing good solutions in complex environment	(a) Tuning of variables is hard	Simulated world and Real time

4   Conclusions

For automatic guided vehicles, navigation and trajectory generation are pre- dominantly important. Over the past two decades abundant research has been done in this field. Either its, kinematic, dynamics of actual vehicle or formulation of number of algorithms for path planning, obstacle avoidance etc. With the ever growing interest, this field is unavoidable in daily activities as they are intelligent systems; who does not need any human assistance. The journey started off from numerical approach has now been shifted towards the stochastic approach. Where finding a solution is guaranteed. The article comprehensively summarizes the latest work done in the field of terrestrial, aerial and undersea for autonomous vehicles. Certain benefits of latest approaches and their drawbacks have been mentioned in the Table 1. Different stochastic algorithms, & deterministic methods are also discussed.

References

1. Abhishek, B., Ranjit, S., Shankar, T., Eappen, G., Sivasankar, P., Rajesh, A.: Hybrid PSO-HSA and PSO-GA algorithm for 3D path planning in autonomous UAVs. SN Appl. Sci. 2(11), 1–16 (2020)
2. Abualigah, L., Abd Elaziz, M., Sumari, P., Geem, Z.W., Gandomi, A.H.: Reptile search algorithm (RSA): a nature-inspired meta-heuristic optimizer. Expert Syst. Appl. 191, 116158 (2022)

3. Arnold, M., Burgermeister, B., Führer, C., Hippmann, G., Rill, G.: Numerical methods in vehicle system dynamics: state of the art and current developments. Veh. Syst. Dyn. **49**(7), 1159–1207 (2011)
4. Ben-Moshe, B., Landau, Y., Marbel, R., Mishiner, A.: Bio-inspired micro drones. In: 2018 IEEE International Conference on the Science of Electrical Engineering in Israel (ICSEE), pp. 1–5. IEEE (2018)
5. Czyż, Z., Suwala, S., Karpiński, P., Skiba, K.: Numerical analysis of the support platform for an unmanned aerial vehicle. In: Journal of Physics: Conference Series, vol. 2130, p. 012029. IOP Publishing (2021)
6. Erke, S., Bin, D., Yiming, N., Qi, Z., Liang, X., Dawei, Z.: An improved a-star based path planning algorithm for autonomous land vehicles. Int. J. Adv. Robot. Syst. **17**(5), 1729881420962263 (2020)
7. Gill, P.E., Murray, W., Saunders, M.A., Wright, M.H.: User's guide for NPSOL (version 4.0): A fortran package for nonlinear programming. Technical report, STANFORD UNIV CA SYSTEMS OPTIMIZATION LAB (1986)
8. Gul, F., et al.: A centralized strategy for multi-agent exploration. IEEE Access **10**, 126871–126884 (2022)
9. Gul, F., Mir, I., Abualigah, L., Sumari, P., Forestiero, A.: A consolidated review of path planning and optimization techniques: technical perspectives and future directions. Electronics **10**(18), 2250 (2021)
10. Gul, F., Mir, S., Mir, I.: Coordinated multi-robot exploration: Hybrid stochastic optimization approach. In: AIAA SCITECH 2022 Forum, p. 1414 (2022)
11. Gul, F., Rahiman, W., Alhady, S.N., Ali, A., Mir, I., Jalil, A.: Meta-heuristic approach for solving multi-objective path planning for autonomous guided robot using PSO–GWO optimization algorithm with evolutionary programming. J. Ambient. Intell. Humaniz. Comput. **12**(1), 7873–7890 (2021)
12. Herman, P.: Numerical test of underwater vehicle dynamics using velocity controller. In: 2019 12th International Workshop on Robot Motion and Control (RoMoCo), pp. 26–31. IEEE (2019)
13. Hu, Y., Zhao, W., Wang, L.: Vision-based target tracking and collision avoidance for two autonomous robotic fish. IEEE Trans. Industr. Electron. **56**(5), 1401–1410 (2009)
14. Hull, T., Enright, W.H., Jackson, K.: Runge-kutta research at toronto. Appl. Numer. Math. **22**(1–3), 225–236 (1996)
15. Ilango, H.S., Ramanathan, R.: A performance study of bio-inspired algorithms in autonomous landing of unmanned aerial vehicle. Procedia Comput. Sci. **171**, 1449–1458 (2020)
16. Kim, Y., Park, J., Son, W., Yoon, T.: Modified turn algorithm for motion planning based on clothoid curve. Electron. Lett. **53**(24), 1574–1576 (2017)
17. Le, A.V., Nhan, N.H.K., Mohan, R.E.: Evolutionary algorithm-based complete coverage path planning for tetriamond tiling robots. Sensors **20**(2), 445 (2020)
18. Lim, H.S., Chin, C.K., Chai, S., Bose, N.: Online AUV path replanning using quantum-behaved particle swarm optimization with selective differential evolution. Comput. Model. Eng. Sci. **125**(1), 33–50 (2020)
19. Lim, H.S., Fan, S., Chin, C.K., Chai, S., Bose, N., Kim, E.: Constrained path planning of autonomous underwater vehicle using selectively-hybridized particle swarm optimization algorithms. IFAC-PapersOnLine **52**(21), 315–322 (2019)
20. Mansury, E., Nikookar, A., Salehi, M.E.: Artificial bee colony optimization of ferguson splines for soccer robot path planning. In: 2013 First RSI/ISM International Conference on Robotics and Mechatronics (ICRoM), pp. 85–89. IEEE (2013)
21. Mir, I., Eisa, S.A., Taha, H.E., Maqsood, A., Akhtar, S., Islam, T.U.: A stability perspective of bio-inspired UAVs performing dynamic soaring opti mally. Bioinspiration Biomimetics (2021)

22. Mir, I., Maqsood, A., Akhtar, S.: Dynamic modeling & stability analysis of a generic UAV in glide phase. In: MATEC Web of Conferences, vol. 114, p. 01007. EDP Sciences (2017)
23. Ni, J., Wu, L., Fan, X., Yang, S.X.: Bioinspired intelligent algorithm and its applications for mobile robot control: a survey. Comput. Intell. Neurosci. **2016**, 1–1 (2016)
24. Noor, M.A., Noor, K.I., Al-Said, E., Waseem, M.: Some new iterative methods for nonlinear equations. Math. Probl. Eng. **2010** (2010)
25. Owen, M.P., Duffy, S.M., Edwards, M.W.: Unmanned aircraft sense and avoid radar: Surrogate flight testing performance evaluation. In: 2014 IEEE Radar Conference, pp. 0548–0551. IEEE (2014)
26. Poudel, S., Moh, S.: Hybrid path planning for efficient data collection in UAV-aided WSNs for emergency applications. Sensors **21**(8), 2839 (2021)
27. Saied, M., Slim, M., Mazeh, H., Francis, C., Shraim, H.: Unmanned aerial vehicles fleet control via artificial bee colony algorithm. In: 2019 4th Con ference on Control and Fault Tolerant Systems (SysTol), pp. 80–85. IEEE (2019)
28. Sánchez-Ferreira, C., Coelho, L., Ayala, H.V., Farias, M.C., Llanos, C.H.: Bio-inspired optimization algorithms for real underwater image restoration. Signal Process. Image Commun. **77**, 49–65 (2019)
29. Sanchez-Lopez, J.L., Wang, M., Olivares-Mendez, M.A., Molina, M., Voos, H.: A real-time 3D path planning solution for collision-free navigation of multirotor aerial robots in dynamic environments. J. Intell. Rob. Syst. **93**(1–2), 33–53 (2019)
30. Shen, C., Shi, Y., Buckham, B.: Model predictive control for an AUV with dynamic path planning. In: 2015 54th Annual Conference of the Society of Instrument and Control Engineers of Japan (SICE), pp. 475–480. IEEE (2015)
31. Szczepanski, R., Erwinski, K., Tejer, M., Bereit, A., Tarczewski, T.: Optimal scheduling for palletizing task using robotic arm and artificial bee colony algorithm. Eng. Appl. Artif. Intell. **113**, 104976 (2022)
32. Szczepanski, R., Tarczewski, T., Erwinski, K.: Energy efficient local path planning algorithm based on predictive artificial potential field. IEEE Access **10**, 39729–39742 (2022)
33. Usman, M.R., Usman, M.A., Yaq, M.A., Shin, S.Y.: UAV reconnaissance using bio-inspired algorithms: Joint PSO and penguin search optimization algorithm (PESOA) attributes. In: 2019 16th IEEE Annual Consumer Com- munications & Networking Conference (CCNC), pp. 1–6. IEEE (2019)
34. Verbeke, J., Cools, R.: The newton-raphson method. Int. J. Math. Educ. Sci. Technol. **26**(2), 177–193 (1995)
35. Wood, G.R.: The bisection method in higher dimensions. Math. Program. **55**(1–3), 319–337 (1992)
36. Yilmaz, N.K., Evangelinos, C., Lermusiaux, P.F., Patrikalakis, N.M.: Path planning of autonomous underwater vehicles for adaptive sampling using mixed integer linear programming. IEEE J. Oceanic Eng. **33**(4), 522–537 (2008)
37. Zhang, K., Sprinkle, J., Sanfelice, R.G.: A hybrid model predictive controller for path planning and path following. In: Proceedings of the ACM/IEEE Sixth International Conference on Cyber-Physical Systems, pp. 139–148 (2015)
38. Zhang, X., Xia, S., Zhang, T., Li, X.: Hybrid FWPS cooperation algorithm based unmanned aerial vehicle constrained path planning. Aerosp. Sci. Technol. **118**, 107004 (2021)
39. Zhang, Y., Guan, G., Pu, X.: The robot path planning based on improved artificial fish swarm algorithm. Mathematical Problems in Engineering **2016** (2016)
40. Zhao, Y.J.: Optimal patterns of glider dynamic soaring. Op- timal control applications and methods **25**(2), 67–89 (2004). https://doi.org/10.1002/oca.739
41. Zhu, D., Li, W., Yan, M., Yang, S.X.: The path planning of AUV based on ds information fusion map building and bio-inspired neural network in unknown dynamic environment. Int. J. Adv. Rob. Syst. **11**(3), 34 (2014)

Author Index

A

Abualigah, Laith   96, 111
Abualigah, Sayel   96
Almahmoud, Mothanna   96

B

Bodrunova, Svetlana   65

C

Cantini, Riccardo   41
Caroprese, Luciano   57
Cassavia, Nunziato   83
Caviglione, Luca   83
Comito, Carmela   57

F

Forestiero, Agostino   96, 111, 125

G

Ghasemi, Mojtaba   111
Guarascio, Massimo   83
Gul, Faiza   125
Gul, Uzma   125

H

Hanandeh, Essam S.   96
Hemmati, Rasul   111

L

Liguori, Angelica   83
Lo Scudo, Fabrizio   17

M

Marozzo, Fabrizio   41
Mir, Imran   125

S

Sachdeva, Gagan   96
Surace, Giuseppe   83

V

Vocaturo, Eugenio   3
Volkovskii, Daniil   65

Z

Zahedi, Amir   111
Zare, Mohsen   111
Zumpano, Ester   3, 57
Zuppelli, Marco   83

C. Comito and D. Talia (Eds.): PerSOM 2022, LNICST 494, p. 139, 2023.
https://doi.org/10.1007/978-3-031-31469-8

Printed in the United States
by Baker & Taylor Publisher Services